Revise for PE GCSE: Edexcel

Second edition

Tony Scott

Heinemann is an imprint of Pearson Education Limited,
a company incorporated in England and Wales, having
its registered office at Edinburgh Gate, Harlow, Essex, CM20 2JE.
Registered company number: 872828

Heinemann is a registered trademark of Pearson Education Limited

First published in 2001
Second edition 2002

08
10 9 8

British Library Cataloguing in Publication Data
A catalogue record for this book is available from the British Library

ISBN: 978 0 435100 42 1

Typeset by Techtype, Abingdon, Oxon
Printed and bound in China (CTPS/08)

Acknowledgements
The publishers would like to thank the following for permission use photographs. Action-
Plus/Chris Barry for the photograph appearing on p.3, Action-Plus/Glyn Kirk on p.4, Action-
Plus/Mike Hewitt on p.18 (top), Empics/Neal Simpson on p.18 (centre), Empics/Tony Marshall on
p.18 (bottom), Empics/Laurence Griffiths on p.19, Empics/David Worthy on p.21,
P. Phillips/SPI on p.26 (left), CNRI/SPL on p.26 (centre), David Scharf/SPI on p.26 (right), Associated
Press/Rob Griffith on p.52 (left), Action-Plus/Neil Tingle on p.52 (centre), Empics/Tony Marshall on
p.52 (right), Empics Sports Agency on p.55 (top and bottom), Action Plus on p.55 (centre), Action
Plus on p.66 (left), Getty on p.66 (right), Empics/Mike Egerton on p.71, Allsport on p.74.

The publishers have made every effort to contact copyright holders. However, if any material
has been incorrectly acknowledged, the publishers would be pleased to correct this at the
earliest opportunity.

Cover photographs by Action-Plus (canoeing picture), Alan Edwards (basketball picture), Image
Bank (swimming picture) and Pictor International (high jump picture)
Illustrations by Catherine Ward Illustrations and Techtype

Tel: 01865 888058 www.heinemann.co.uk

Contents

How to use this book

This book has been written especially for students who are taking any Edexcel GCSE Physical Education specification. It contains only the basic information on the specification to ensure that you can answer any question set on any aspect of it. For more detailed coverage use *GCSE PE for Edexcel*. This deals in more detail with the specification content and the issues raised by it.

As there are two different specifications, before you start to revise make sure you are absolutely clear about which one you are taking.

- Physical Education (1827)
- Physical Education – Short Course (3827)

If you are taking the long course (1827) you will need to revise every topic in this revision book as, in one way or another, they will all be examined. If you are taking the short course check against the specification which parts are included, and make a list of them before starting to revise. The exact specification part can then be matched up with the sections of this book.

The book is written in a particular sequence in order to show how the specification and the subject of Physical Education fit together as a whole, and is more than the sum of its constituent parts. To learn the specification parts in isolation will enable you to deal well with the knowledge recall type questions, but in order to get the higher grades (A and A*) you must **understand** and be able to **explain** how the parts fit together. If you learn anatomy and physiology in isolation you will not be able to cope with the application of this knowledge in the scenario type questions that are used to differentiate higher calibre students.

How to use this book
The best way to use the book is to:

1. Read the topic.
2. Check the topic box to make sure you know the topic.

3. Do the questions.
4. Check your answers against those at the end of the book.
5. Read the topic again if you have any wrong answers (most of the questions are set in the order that the topic is read).

How each chapter is organised
For this topic you should study
These boxes will give you the main points of the topic and will therefore enable you to find any particular point you wish to revise quickly. This will also be helpful for your final revision session in highlighting specific points.

Definitions
These include all the terms you will need for the examination for the Edexcel specification.

Did you know?
These are extra pieces of information, often useful to give as examples in the examination.

Hints and tips
These can help in two ways: first, as points to know for the examination, and second, as a trigger for certain points that are often not done well in the examination.

Test yourself questions
The questions at the end of each topic are very similar to those you can expect to find in the examination paper, so if you do well on a section in the book you should be able to do well on that section in the examination. For many of the questions you will need to refer back to the profiles on pages 1 and 2.

Answers to questions
Answers are provided to all the 'Test yourself' questions and these can be traced back to where they appear in the book to re-check.

Examination preparation
There is a final section on how to prepare for the examination, and a number of tips on how to remember answers and tackle questions.

Section A: Factors affecting participation in physical activity

1 Reasons for taking part in physical activity

For this topic you should study:
- your reasons for taking part in sport
- the reasons why others take part in sport
- physical, social and mental reasons.

Reasons why people take part in sport come under three main categories: physical, social and mental. Read the profiles set out for the people below, and study their reasons for taking part in sport and physical activity.

Task

Draw a table like the one below. Write reasons for taking part in sport for each of the profiles in the correct columns. Most of these are highlighted for you.

Name	Physical	Social	Mental
Garry (16)	challenge	competitive	enjoys

Garry (16) is waiting to start as a YTS footballer with a first division club. He loves (*enjoys*) playing football, especially the physical nature of the game (*challenge*) and he is very *competitive*.

Derek (50) is an ex-champion who has always been very fit. Though he no longer competes at the highest level, he knows that being fit contributes to *good health* and well-being (*look and feel good*). He follows a Personal Exercise Programme (PEP) and has joined a golf club that enables him to *socialise*. He takes regular skiing holidays, a sport that he finds particularly *stimulating*.

Teresa (50) is a grandmother and non-sportswoman. She does aerobics four times a week because it *keeps her fit* and helps her to *look and feel good*. She goes with a group of friends as this helps her *social life*.

Elaine (34) has a new, high-powered job at a university. She *enjoys* swimming and has started a swimming programme. She trains with some colleagues and this has helped her to settle into her job (*improves co-operation*). She also finds that exercise *relieves stress and tension* and contributes to *good health*.

Jack (56) is an ex-sportsman who is recovering from a serious operation. He follows a PEP that involves weight training, flexibility and running. After losing a lot of muscle (atrophy) through illness, the training is helping to *improve his body shape* and contributing to his *rehabilitation* and *good health.*

Task

Look carefully at the profiles that follow and write down at least three reasons these people might have for taking part in sport. An example has been done for you.

Name	Physical	Social	Mental
Lionel (39)	physical challenge	develops friendships	relieves stress

Luke (20): a national champion in his sport.

Matt C (18): competes at national level in his sport.

Matt S (26): an ex-national champion in his sport, still follows a PEP.

Ian (30): an ex-footballer, follows a PEP (running and weights programme).

Duncan (23): football referee.

Norbert (74): non-sportsman, does light weights and exercise bicycle programme.

Albert (92): runs in the London Marathon every year.

Jill (42): an ex-netball player, runs cross-country.

Audrey (40): an ex-international swimmer, swims and works out in the gym.

Anita (66): a non-sportswoman but now swims and line dances.

Louise (44): an ex-badminton player, does weights and exercise bicycle programme.

Ann (46): a non-sportswoman, does weights, step and exercise programme.

Barrie (50): an ex-footballer, runs every day.

Lionel (39): an ex-rugby player, follows a weights programme and plays golf.

Alan (40): another ex-rugby player, overweight, no exercise, unfit, unhappy.

Now write down your own profile fully, stating at least three reasons you have for taking part in sport and physical activity. In brackets state which of the three categories they come into – for example, improve my body shape (physical). Then set them out in a table like the one above.

• *Sport relieves stress and tension.*

• *Some people enjoy sport.*

• *Joining a fitness club can help you to make new friends.*

Hints and Tips

In the examination you will need to be able to relate the reasons for taking part in sport to a certain profile. Make sure you can adapt the reasons you have learned for different types of sports people.

Assets that make a champion

For this topic you should study:
- assets that make a sports champion
- factors that affect performance
- skill-related fitness (see pages 79 and 80)
- factors of health-related exercise.

Different assets for different sports

There are many factors that affect both participation and performance. These will be examined in your GCSE course and are covered in the following pages. The factors that affect performance at the highest levels of sport vary according to the sport and the sports person taking part. These factors may affect the position that a player plays in, or they may affect the style that the player adopts. For example, in basketball the tall players (**body build** is a factor) will play nearer to the ring at each end of the court so that they can rebound the ball from the backboard, while the smaller players will set up the plays (**speed** will be a factor). In athletics, Marion Jones, the world's fastest female sprinter (in the year 2000), has speed and power, while Denise Lewis, a heptathlete (seven events) has to combine speed over 100 metres and **endurance** over 800 metres with the more technical skills needed for the high jump and javelin which are included in her event. She will also need **strength** combined with speed in the shot and these two together form another factor, **power**.

More than one way to the top of the mountain

Different physical activities and sports require different factors for success – or the same factors but in different amounts. The great athlete Daley Thompson once said, 'There is more than one way to the top of the mountain!' – although one sports person may reach the highest levels of a sport with certain skills, others may reach the same levels using different skills.

Hints and Tips
There are six skill-related fitness factors (motor skills):
- agility
- co-ordination
- reaction time
- balance
- power
- speed.

Task

For the sportsman illustrated in the photograph here take the six skill-related fitness factors and list them in the order of importance. (Skill factors are dealt with in detail on pages 79 and 80.)

There are many other factors that affect participation and performance. Some of these are not concerned with **skill fitness** or physical fitness but may be more to do with a performer's social background or the psychological aspects that are so important in sport today. You may know of sports people or play in a team which has players who may not be the most gifted in terms of actual talent (skill fitness) but who make up for this lack of natural ability in other ways – for example, hard work, determination or a great desire to succeed at their sport. In the same way you may know of sports people who have squandered their natural ability. Where some may have given up, others who are stronger psychologically may have succeeded. Some may have been adversely influenced by less talented team-mates or friends, or lacked the influence of a good coach or access to good facilities. Others may have overcome many setbacks, injuries and disappointments. These are all factors that affect participation and performance, but in this course you are most concerned with those that come under the headings of physical fitness, **health-related exercise** (including anatomy and physiology), and skill fitness.

Hints and Tips
Make sure you understand the different categories under which the factors affecting participation and performance occur:
- *skill fitness*
- *health-related exercise*
- *psychological*
- *physical fitness*
- *social.*

Tasks

1. Many sports people are adversely affected by, or come under the influence of, others. These are often friends, team-mates or even family. Give examples of this from a variety of sports and explain the adverse factors you think might have influenced potentially great players.

2. For the sportswoman illustrated in the photograph, list the six skill-related fitness factors in order of importance. Compare this list with the one you made on the previous page.

3. Take a look at your own best sport and write down in order of importance the skill-related factors of performance as they relate to your sport.

4. Take a look at your performance in this sport, then write down the three skills in which you perform best and the three in which you perform least well.

5. Analyse your performance in your best three skills.

6. How can you improve in the three skills in which you perform least well?

Hints and Tips
Diego Maradona is an example of a great player whose performance has often been adversely affected by off-the-field controversy. Drugs, late nights and lack of fitness are some of the factors that affected his performance.

Health, exercise, fitness and performance

For this topic you should study:
- health, exercise, fitness, and performance
- hygiene, athlete's foot, verrucae.

Whether you are a champion, aspiring champion, ex-champion or just interested in being fit and healthy, **health**, **exercise**, **fitness** and **performance** are very important factors in achieving your goals. As a student you will need to know these terms and be able to use them accurately in the examination.

Health

> ### Definition
> Health is a state of complete psychological, physical and social well-being, not simply the absence of disease or infirmity.

There have been a number of sports people who have reached the top in their sports and yet they have, in the strict terms of this definition of health, not been healthy. Blindness is an infirmity, but one blind female American athlete represented America in the Sydney Olympics 2000.

Exercise

> ### Definition
> Exercise is a form of physical activity done primarily to improve one's health and physical fitness.

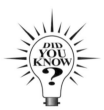

You can be fit but not necessarily healthy. Steven Redgrave, five times Olympic champion gold medalist, suffers from diabetes and ulcerative colitis.

All top sports persons know the importance of exercise for their own particular sport. The nature and type of exercise might differ from one sport to another and sports people within the same sport may undertake different forms of exercise. In golf there is a wide variety of different types of body shape among players performing at the top level (a point we will come to later). Players also exercise differently – indeed, some exercise very rarely. This may change: currently Tiger Woods dominates the sport at all the major tournaments, and he trains very hard.

Exercise is not just for the champions and top sports performers, it is for everyone. It is not one specific activity – just running or just swimming, for example. Exercise is a form of physical activity and as such covers a wide variety of activities that include indoor exercise, outdoor exercise, individual exercise, exercise with a partner, team games, competitive exercise and non-competitive exercise. You can exercise in one specific way or a variety of different ways.

Although there are many professional sports persons, teachers of sport and coaches, exercise is done primarily to improve health and fitness. For this reason there are many campaigns run by governments and other agencies to encourage people to take part in physical activity, and it is also why health-related exercise is a compulsory part of the National Curriculum for students in schools.

Fitness

Definition
Fitness is the ability to meet the demands of the environment.

Fitness is another important aspect for athletes in sport. We often read about sports people who are unfit to take part in a competition or who are not at their peak level of fitness. Fitness also means being able (fit) to do the work, play and everyday aspects of your normal life without any undue repercussions. These repercussions might, for example, mean that after participating in a marathon, you are unable to go to work or school the next day or, after work or school not being able to enjoy your free time.

Performance

Definition
Performance is how well a task is completed.

Performance is the final act following the preparation, training and participation (and, in sport, would be followed by recovery and cool down). Although it is a term often used in sport, it can also refer to activities such as music or drama. It can also be applied to activities related to simply being or getting fit, and could certainly apply to all the characters in the profiles on pages 1 and 2.

In order to give their best performance, opera singers warm up.

Hygiene

Definition
Hygiene is a term relating to the principles of maintaining good health.

It is important in sport and fitness training to maintain good hygiene, to wear specialist sports or training clothing and footwear, to shower to remove sweat and body odours, to dry carefully, and to use powder and/or deodorant. Finally, you should change into fresh clothing, especially underwear, after participation in competition or training activities. Good hygiene is also needed to prevent specific problems that often affect sports persons, namely athlete's foot and verrucae.

Athlete's foot
Athlete's foot is a fungal infection that causes dry, flaky skin between the toes. It is infectious – that is, it can be passed on from one person to another. In exercise and sport it can be passed on through sharing towels, socks and training shoes, or by walking barefoot in swimming pools or shower areas. It can be treated with a special powder and/or cream.

Verrucae
Verrucae are normally found on the sole of the foot and are also known as plantar warts. They are caused by a virus. These too are often passed on through the environment of a swimming pool, so if you have a verruca it is necessary to wear a special sock to prevent passing it on. A small operation may be needed to remove a verruca, although sometimes they can be treated with liquid nitrogen.

Test yourself

Reasons for taking part in physical activity

1. In the definition for health there are three aspects regarding a person's well-being. Write out these three aspects as column headings in a table. **3 marks**

2. From the five main profiles on pages 1 and 2 choose one *reason for taking part* for each of your headings in question 1. Write each one of your chosen *reason for taking part* along with the name of the profile character in the relevant column in your table. **3 marks**

3. Select three of the profile characters on pages 1 and 2 for whom exercise **is not done** primarily for health and fitness. **3 marks**

4. Select four of the profile characters for whom exercise **is done** primarily for health and fitness. **4 marks**

5. The definition for fitness includes the words 'meet the demands of the environment'. Give two examples of what is meant by this. **2 marks**

6. What might be the repercussions of not being fit for the ordinary person? **1 mark**

7. Performance can be used not only to describe something competitive but also something related to training. Describe an example of performance with respect to a training session. **1 mark**

8. Give full definitions of health, exercise, fitness and performance. **4 marks**

9. Hygiene is very important to all those who take part in sport. Explain two important aspects of good hygiene that all sports people should keep to. **2 marks**

10. All of the sports people illustrated in the profiles are at risk from both verrucae and athlete's foot. One of these conditions is a virus while the other is a fungal infection. Which is which? **2 marks**

11. A verruca is also known by another name. What is it? **1 mark**

12. Describe how athlete's foot can be recognised, how it can be treated and how it can be passed on to another person. **3 marks**

13. In what sort of environment are verrucae most likely to be passed on? **1 mark**

Total 30 marks

2 Body composition

For this topic you should study:
- health-related exercise
- body composition
- the effects of under and overeating.

Health related exercise

Health related exercise is a complete and distinct area of Physical Education that is sub-divided into five areas: cardiovascular fitness, muscular strength, muscular endurance, flexibility and **body composition**. It is important to be able to recognise health related exercise terms as opposed to skill-related fitness, as these terms are sometimes muddled up. Each of the five health related exercise areas is important in its own right and each contributes to a person's health in a different way.

Body composition

Definition
Body composition is defined as the percentage of body weight that is fat, muscle and bone.

Body weight is an aspect of general fitness. The topic of body weight regularly features in the media for two reasons: being too fat (that is, too much of a person's body weight is fat), or being too thin. There are a number of different ways to work out the ideal weight of someone, taking into consideration his/her body build or body shape. Ideal weight is known as a person's **optimum weight**.

Hints and Tips
- *Learn the definition for body composition.*
- *Identify ways of improving it.*
- *Remember that optimum weight is the most favourable weight for that person.*

Why optimum weight may vary

It is quite possible for two people of the same height to weigh different amounts, but both to be at their optimum weight. For example, if one were male and one were female, we would have to consider that men are usually more heavily boned and muscled, while women have an extra layer of fat. However, if we compared two men or two women, we would have to consider their bone structure. A simple comparison of their wrist girth might give an indication of this component. Even if they were of comparable bone structure, one could be more muscular and this might be the reason for the difference in weight.

This is because different parts of our body composition weigh differently. Muscle and bone are heavy, so an athlete with well-developed muscles might appear to be overweight when compared to a non-athlete who is not heavily muscled or does not have a heavy bone structure. Similarly, when compared to a person who is very fat, but who has less muscle and a smaller bone structure, the athlete may be of similar weight, but one will be **overweight** and the other **overfat**. If they are grossly overweight, they could be **obese**.

It is rare in sport for an overfat person to excel, but sumo wrestlers need to be overfat.

The question of a person's age will also come into the equation as this factor has an influence on optimum weight. As we get older, we lose muscle mass, some people lose bone density and we even get shorter. These factors will have an effect on our optimum body weight.

We have identified three important terms that are closely linked to body composition: overweight, overfat and obese. On this occasion, we have looked in some detail at each component before establishing their definitions. You should now be able to understand the definitions more easily.

Definitions
Overweight is defined as having weight in excess of normal, not harmful unless accompanied by overfatness.

Overfat is the term used to describe a person who has too much body composition as fat; men having more than 19% of total body composition as fat and women having more than 26%.

Obese is the term used to describe extremely overweight, often considered as 20% to 35% above normal, probably best described as an extreme overfat condition.

Hints and Tips
Learn to explain why optimum weight varies according to weight, sex, age, height, bone structure and muscle girth (the measurement around the circumference of our muscles).

The effects of under/overeating on body weight and performance

One of the main aspects concerning body composition is diet. This is a major factor that affects not only sports people but all people whether they are aspiring champion athletes, whether they want to be fit, whether they are unfit, or whether they are undernourished because they do not have enough to eat (as is the case for much of the world's population).

Diet and sport

We should not consider diet as simply a way of eating in order to lose weight. Everyone has a diet of some sort and we can consider three of our profile characters in this respect. Luke (20) is a national throwing champion, 6'4" tall and 15 stones in weight, heavily boned and muscled, with no excess fat, but not yet heavy enough to reach his full potential. Matt C is 18 and competes at middle distance in the National Schools Championships. He is 5'9" tall and weighs under 10 stones. Garry, aged 16, wants to be a professional footballer. He is 5'9" tall and nearly 11 stones, well muscled with no excess fat. All of these potential future champions need different diets.

Energy balance

Weight loss, weight gain or keeping your weight constant are regulated by balancing the amount and type of food you eat with the amount of energy you use up during work, rest and play. This is known as **energy balance**, and is calculated in kilocalories (or calories). The above three profile characters each need a balanced diet specific to their particular needs.

There are three ways of losing weight:

- decreasing kilocalorie intake
- increasing kilocalorie energy expenditure
- using a combination of both.

Eating the right diet

Our three potential champions need different balanced diets to suit their particular sport. In fact we might go further and say that, in some cases, their diet might depend upon the position they play. For example, Garry is a mid-field player and uses up a lot of energy compared to a goalkeeper. However, he still needs to be strong and to develop muscle. Luke needs to be very strong and powerful, so the extra weight will help him to achieve this. Matt C does not want extra weight to carry around the track but needs to be strong enough for his event.

> *Hints and Tips*
> *Make sure you are able to explain why an individual's diet depends on body type and the sport for which that individual is training.*

Optimum weight for specific sports

Optimum weight can also be related to specific sports, and to the position that a player plays in a particular sport. We will consider below the effects of under or overeating on body weight and performance. It would not be unusual to look at a shot putter, male or female, and see that they are usually overweight, but not necessarily overfat. Until recent years they might well have been overfat too, but present-day shot putters have a much more **athletic** build.

At the opposite end of the spectrum are the jockeys and long-distance runners who are often very thin for their height and underweight compared to most people of similar height and build.

Effects of undereating

Throwers usually reach their peak at a later age than sprinters, and in throwing events competitors cannot afford to be underweight. This means that throwers need to eat a lot so that they can convert this energy into muscle, and therefore become more powerful and throw further. Similarly, Sumo wrestlers would certainly be considered obese by normal standards, but they have to eat to keep up their weight, because being underweight would be a distinct disadvantage. Jockeys and distance runners have the opposite problem as they are already underweight by normal standards and so extreme undereating for them can lead to the eating disorder **anorexia nervosa**.

Effects of overeating

The effect of overeating for the Sumo wrestler is that the extra fat is considered a health risk because of the dangers relating to heart disease. For the jockeys and distance runners the extra weight gain from overeating would mean a distinct disadvantage in their sport. These are extreme situations, but overeating in particular can affect the performance of many sports people. Footballers and boxers make headlines if they are thought to be 'carrying too much weight'. The reason in their case is almost always that the loss of speed and agility affects their ability to perform at their previous levels, when they were at their optimum body weight. Perhaps the best example in recent years has been the loss of form of tennis star Andre Agassi in 1999. Overfat and unfit, he was knocked out in the first round of the Australian Championships in January, but fit and playing great tennis at his optimum weight he won the French title in August of the same year!

Hints and Tips
Be able to explain how optimum body weight can affect performance.

Test yourself

Body composition

1. In addition to body composition list the other four aspects of health-related exercise. **4 marks**

2. The fifth component of health-related exercise is body composition. Define this term. **1 mark**

3. Optimum weight means the ideal weight for a person considering certain factors. Give three examples of the factors that might affect this. **3 marks**

4. Consider the profiles of Audrey and Louise on page 2. If these two women were the same height explain why their optimum weight might be different. **2 marks**

5. Luke could be described as being overweight. However, in his case it is not a harmful condition. Why might this be? **1 mark**

6. Alan is unfit and at least two stones above his optimum weight, so he could be described as overfat. Define the term overfat. **1 mark**

7. If Alan were extremely overfat, what term would be used to describe him? **1 mark**

8. Consider the three profile characters Luke, Garry and Matt C. Explain what the effects of overeating might be on each of them. Do not use the same reason more than once. **3 marks**

9. Alan cannot keep to his optimum weight now he has stopped training and playing sport, so he needs to lose weight. What are the three ways he can do this? **3 marks**

10. Study the profiles of Albert, Jill and Barrie. Relating back to your previous answer, explain why you think each of them might be underweight. **1 mark**

11. In a game such as tennis, being overfat would affect the performance of the player considerably, as was seen in the case of Andre Agassi in 1999 (described on page 11). Using this example, give three reasons why his performance might have been made worse by the fact that he was not at his optimum weight. **3 marks**

12. In some areas of sport, sports people find it necessary to undereat in order to be able to compete at the highest levels, or in some cases to be allowed to compete at all. Give an example of a sport where the sports person might undereat in order to improve his/her performance. **1 mark**

13. Give an example of it being necessary to keep to a very strict diet (often undereating) in order to compete in a sport. **1 mark**

Total 25 marks

3 Diet

For this topic you should study:
- the seven factors of a balanced diet
- diet and potential.

The seven factors of a balanced diet

Optimum body weight is important, energy balance is important, it is important not to be underweight and it is important not to be overweight in order to stay healthy and compete in sport. Therefore, it is important to have a balanced **diet**. There are seven main factors of a balanced diet and it is important to understand the correct proportion for each of these factors.

Carbohydrates

We have already discussed the importance of energy balance. To lose weight you need less energy in (in the way of food) and/or more energy out (in the way of exercise). We can take energy in from three food sources – **carbohydrates**, **fat** and **protein**. However, our main energy source should be from carbohydrates. All of our profile characters need to take in carbohydrates to maintain their energy because they use a lot of energy in their physical activities. There are two types of carbohydrate:

- sugar (simple)
- starch (complex).

Almost half of our energy should come from foods like bread, pasta, potatoes and rice (complex carbohydrates). Sweets and chocolate contain simple carbohydrates, but they also contain fat. After eating carbohydrate we store it in the liver as a substance called **glycogen**, which can easily be converted into **glucose** and used as energy in the muscles, brain and other organs when needed. After we compete or train we need to replace the energy we have used.

Fats

Everyone needs to eat fat because it contains energy and also helps to make other things work such as fat-soluble **vitamins**. The amount of energy we get from fats should be much less than we get from carbohydrates; no more than 30% is the recommended amount. The energy provided by fat is burned up when we exercise over longer periods – for example, when running a marathon.

Proteins

Although protein can be used as an energy source (about half of that provided by fat), it is mainly needed to build and repair muscle and tissue. Protein is therefore important to sports people in a number of respects because they need it to grow and to be strong for competition; they also need it to repair damaged tissue and to recover from injury. It is important to use proteins and carbohydrates, as they are stored as fat if not used in other ways. Animal protein comes from meat, fish, milk, cheese and eggs. Plant protein comes from vegetables, cereals, pasta and rice.

Vitamins

Many people get their vitamins in tablet form, but a balanced diet will also provide all the vitamins required by the body, as we only need them in small amounts. Vitamins can be found in dairy products, fresh vegetables, meat, cereals, nuts, fruit and vegetable oil. We need vitamins for a variety of reasons – for example, they help our vision, skin, bones, teeth, healing capability and many more things.

Minerals

There are numerous minerals that need to be included in a balanced diet, and they all have a particular function. **Calcium** and **iron** are two of the most important ones and are mentioned here because they appear in a different context in other parts of the course. It is important to understand how these minerals are required by everyone, including the specialist needs of sports people.

Calcium is important for teeth, but it is also important in the development and growth of bones in the young and in maintaining bone density in the old.

Iron is important because it is a constituent of **haemoglobin** and is required for the formation of red blood cells. It is therefore important in controlling the amount of oxygen our blood can contain, and in this respect it is important to everyone – in particular, long-distance athletes.

Water

Water is used to transport nutrients, waste and hormones. It is most important for sports people participating in endurance events and activities of long duration such as the Tour de France, the London Marathon and long boxing matches where the athletes and performers sweat profusely. Without water such athletes would become dehydrated.

Fibre

Wholegrain cereals and bread provide insoluble fibre that bulks our food and helps to prevent constipation. Fruit and vegetables provide soluble fibre that helps to reduce blood cholesterol levels.

Hints and Tips
- *Understand the nutritional requirements of a balanced diet and the importance and use of carbohydrates, fats, proteins, vitamins, minerals, water and fibre.*
- *Understand the importance of protein and water and how they affect performance.*

Diet and potential

It is important to take your diet seriously in order to reach your potential in sport. There are some simple rules that we can use to keep a balanced diet.

- It is important to start the day with breakfast in order to provide energy to get through the day, and also to make sure that your intake of complex carbohydrates is emphasised as opposed to the simple carbohydrates found in sweets and chocolate.
- If it is necessary to diet to lose weight this should be done gradually by reducing the amount of fat you eat, especially that found on meat.
- The best way to stay at your optimum weight is to keep to a balanced diet, making sure that the amount of energy you put into your body is equalled by the amount of energy you use up in the form of exercise. This is known as energy balance.

How we use our energy

As we have seen, most of our energy comes from carbohydrates. We use this energy for all activities, competition or training that are of a high intensity and short duration – events such as the 100 metres in athletics, sprint swimming, a fast break in basketball or a javelin throw.

When the activity, training or competition has a lower intensity and takes place over a longer time period (up to two hours in duration), such as a football match, a hockey match or a volleyball game, energy is provided by carbohydrates and fat in equal amounts.

When the exercise is over a longer time period than two hours, the amount of energy derived from the fat stores will increase. The marathon is a good example, as runners often undergo what is known as **carbo-loading**. This is a method of getting more carbohydrates into their energy stores by trying to fool the body by starving it of carbohydrate for a few days, then loading it in the days just prior to the race.

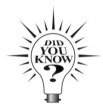

You should eat a light meal high in carbohydrate at least two hours before training or competing.

Hints and Tips
- *Understand the energy requirements for your sport, and know where the energy in your diet comes from.*
- *Remember to drink plenty of water or energy drinks, especially if you exercise or take part in sport.*

Test yourself

Diet

1. There are seven factors of a balanced diet, all of which are needed for various reasons. Carbohydrates are one source of energy. Name the correct terms to describe two types of carbohydrate (other than simple and complex).   **2 marks**

2. Match the terms *simple* and *complex* to your answers from the previous question.   **2 marks**

3. Norbert (74) likes cake. Which form of carbohydrate does this come under?   **1 mark**

4. Matt C (18) is an 800m runner and gets most of his carbohydrate from pasta. Which type of carbohydrate is this?   **1 mark**

5. Give an example of an alternative Matt C might use to pasta in his diet.   **1 mark**

6. All of the profile characters need energy from carbohydrates, but which of the two types listed in your answer to question 2 is the most important for them?   **1 mark**

7. Because of the type of event he does (throwing), Luke (20) would emphasise a different factor in his diet. Which factor might this be? Why would he need to emphasise this factor? Give an example of a suitable food source of this factor.   **3 marks**

8. Several of our profile characters are conscious of their weight. Which of the three energy factors should they cut down on to lose weight?   **1 mark**

9. We get our energy from three main food sources – carbohydrates, fats and proteins. Link these percentages with the correct food source: 15%, 47%, 30%.   **3 marks**

10. Most people can get their vitamin requirements from a balanced diet, but how can they supplement their vitamin intake?   **1 mark**

11. There are many minerals that we need in a balanced diet. Calcium is one and iron another. Give one example of how we use each of these.   **2 marks**

12. In Luke's throwing event, which of the food groups would he get his energy from?   **1 mark**

13. Albert (92) is very fit for his age, but when he runs the marathon it takes him over five hours. Explain briefly how he might store up on carbohydrate energy for the race.   **2 marks**

14. What other type of energy stores might Albert call on in a race over such a long time?   **1 mark**

15. Why does Albert drink plenty of water during the race?   **1 mark**

16. There is one food factor remaining for a balanced diet. State which it is and explain why it is important.   **2 marks**

Total 25 marks

4 Somatotypes

For this topic you should study:

- somatotype and sports potential
- endomorph
- mesomorph
- ectomorph.

Somatotype

> **Definition**
> Somatotype is the technical term for body type, also referred to as body build or physique.

There are three dominant somatotypes (body types) – **endomorph, mesomorph** and **ectomorph** – and we all have different amounts of each. Not only can body type affect performance but also the sport a person plays. In some sports, it can affect the position the person plays and his/her health and fitness.

Measuring body type

Body type can be measured by studying photographs of people, but it is usually measured by taking into account a person's height, weight, bone size, muscle girth and fat content, so somatotyping is very much concerned with all the aspects of body composition we have looked at earlier in the book. Once these measurements have been taken, the person is given a score out of seven for each component – endomorph (or fat score), mesomorph (or muscle score) and ectomorph (or score for thinness). These components are always referred to in this order when giving a body type and they are written as 2:6:2, for example. This would indicate 2/7 for fat, 6/7 for muscle and 2/7 for thinness. We would therefore expect a person with this score to look muscular, athletic and strong. This body type is likely to be found in many professional sports people, especially those needing strength.

Many people have a body type that is a combination of muscle and fat or muscle and thinness, with one slightly dominant feature. A somatotype of 4:5:1, for example, would mean this type was dominant in muscle but tending to be fat. This body type would be called a mesomorphic endomorph. If the second most dominant feature was thinness, the type would be a mesomorphic ectomorph.

A person's natural body type is passed on from parents to children in their genes, but it can be changed under certain conditions such as extreme training, diet or drugs.

> ### Hints and Tips
> - *Understand and explain the different body types (somatotypes): endomorph, mesomorph and ectomorph.*
> - *Understand the different combinations of the terms endomorph, mesomorph and ectomorph.*

Endomorphs in sport

Endomorphs are those body types that are predominantly fat. Therefore, the sports in which they dominate often require strength but not stamina, as the person will usually have extra weight to carry. The most obvious sport in which endomorphs are found is Sumo wrestling where weight is of paramount importance and, as the contests usually last a very short time, lack of endurance does not matter as much as in other sports.

Mesomorphs in sport

These are the muscular somatotypes who can usually perform well in a wide variety of sports, especially those where strength and speed are required and also the combination of these two factors, power. These somatotypes are seen in the traditional sports where they have always dominated – for example, sprinting and rowing. They are also found in certain positions in games such as rugby, where they play scrum half or fly half as speed, strength and agility are important. The mesomorph is beginning to dominate at the highest levels in sport, with the endomorphic rugby forward a thing of the past. We also see mesomorphs much more often in games such as tennis and in athletics, where the fat endomorphic shot putters and discus throwers have given way to the big athletic mesomorph.

Ectomorphs in sport

Ectomorphs are the opposite of endomorphs in body type, and the same can be said of their potential in sport. You will rarely find an ectomorph in sports requiring strength. They can usually be found in the endurance events. In general, the longer the race, the thinner the athlete. In fact, many athletes are now often suspected of not eating enough and losing weight deliberately so they can run faster and longer.

Hints and Tips

- *Understand and explain where and how different body types fit into sport.*
- *Understand and explain the effect of body type on performance in sport.*

Where does body type not matter?
A few sports are thought to be suitable for any body type. Golf provides an example of this, where all body types can be found at the top levels of the sport. This may change with the advent of Tiger Woods and other top golfers who follow severe training regimes not witnessed before in this sport and as a result are dominating the game at the highest level.

Somatotype and sports performance

Once a person's somatotype has been established, it can be plotted on a somatochart and compared to other somatotypes. Trends or patterns have shown that certain body types have a distinct suitability to certain types of sports.

Changing a person's body type
Body type can be changed under certain conditions. For example, a change in diet can lead to a change in body build. In later topics we will see that training regimes for strength will also help to change body build, and sometimes when athletes take drugs they too will help to bring about a change in body build. All these are factors that will affect performance in sport.

Hints and Tips
Make sure you understand and are able to explain how body type can be changed.

Summary of body types

Below is a physical description for each of the three body types. Try to build an image of these types in your mind. The diagram will help you.

- Endomorph – short/dumpy with narrow shoulders and broad hips, pear-shaped with a low centre of gravity (helps in some sports – for example, sumo wrestling).
- Mesomorph – broad shoulders with narrow hips; muscular. (A sprinter would have this body shape.)
- Ectomorph – low body weight, tall and thin with a high centre of gravity (helps in some sports – for example, high jump).

Typical somatotypes

Test yourself

Somatotypes

1. The term 'body type' is one way of expressing the body build of a person, but what is the technical term used to describe body type?

    1 mark

2. Give three examples of body composition that are involved with body type/somatotype.

    3 marks

3. There are three components of body type (somatotype). Give the three components in the correct order.

    3 marks

4. A score out of seven is given in each component and the person's somatotype is stated according to the highest score. What would be the somatotype of a person with a score of 1:3:5?

    1 mark

5. When giving a person's score it is also possible to indicate the second dominant feature in order to give a better picture of the body type. Which two words would you use to describe the somatotype 3:6:1 in order to indicate the second feature?

    2 marks

6. If a person is described as an endomorphic mesomorph, what would be the dominant feature of body composition and what would be the second most dominant feature?

    2 marks

7. From the list of sports given below indicate which somatotype you think would be most fitting for each. You could use a combination of somatotypes for some of them.

    8 marks

Sport	Somatotype
Tennis at Wimbledon	
100m sprint (Olympic final)	
Flat race jockey	
Golf (the Open)	
Football (midfielder)	
Basketball (rebounder)	
World's strongest man	
Sumo wrestler	

8. Check the profiles of Luke, Garry and Matt C on pages 1 and 2 and indicate from these descriptions which would be the dominant somatotype for each of them.

    3 marks

9. Read through the profile of Jack on page 2 and state what you think his somatotype would have been before starting his PEP.

    1 mark

10. Which particular part of Jack's PEP would be most responsible for changing his body type?

    1 mark

Total 25 marks

5 Cardiovascular fitness 1

For this topic you should study:
- the heart
- the circulatory system.

The heart

The most important aspect of health-related exercise is **cardiovascular fitness**, which is concerned with the fitness of the heart, the blood and the blood vessels. It is an important factor that affects participation and performance in physical activity. A knowledge and understanding of the workings of the cardiovascular system and how training and fitness affects the heart will enable you to demonstrate the relationship between these two factors.

A knowledge of the heart and an ability to identify each different part is essential, and you must know the route the blood takes when it circulates around the body. This is described on page 22.

The quality and efficiency with which the heart works is a major factor that will affect a person's participation in sport, and the level and quality of the performance he/she is able to give. The fact that Miguel Indurain (see below) had such a low resting heart rate, a massive lung capacity and a strong psychological approach to his sport (never let your opponents see when it is hurting you) all helped him to be such a great champion in his sport.

The cyclist Miguel Indurain, former winner of the Tour de France, had a resting heart rate of 27 beats per minute (BPM) when competing at his highest level.

The circulatory system

The double pump circulatory system

The heart works as a double circulatory pump, and it is important to know and understand how each system works, how they work together and how the two systems are involved with health, exercise, fitness and performance. The heart is divided into two halves by a central partition called the septum. The left half carries oxygenated blood (blood that carries oxygen) and the right half carries de-oxygenated blood. The septum prevents the two different types of blood from mixing and ensures that oxygen is transported out of the heart to the body.

Blood is pumped *away* from the heart by two separate routes. One route takes blood to the lungs and the other to the body (muscles and organs and so on). Each route goes through a valve called a semilunar valve. Any vessel leaving the heart is called an **artery** (the biggest artery is called the **aorta**). Any vessel entering the heart is called a **vein**.

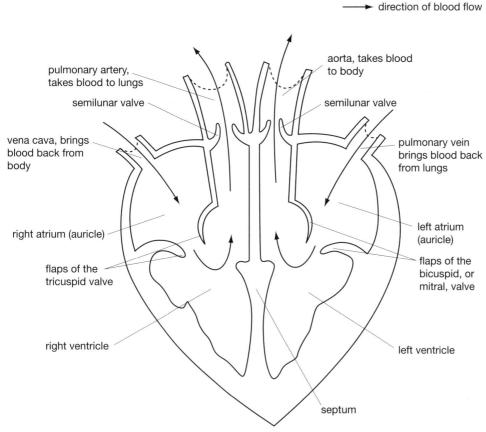

→ direction of blood flow

pulmonary artery, takes blood to lungs

aorta, takes blood to body

semilunar valve

semilunar valve

vena cava, brings blood back from body

pulmonary vein brings blood back from lungs

right atrium (auricle)

left atrium (auricle)

flaps of the tricuspid valve

flaps of the bicuspid, or mitral, valve

right ventricle

left ventricle

septum

The heart

The pulmonary circulatory system

De-oxygenated blood (which carries carbon dioxide and waste products) enters the right **atrium** through the vena cava, then travels through the tricuspid valve into the right **ventricle**. From here it goes through a semilunar valve into the **pulmonary circulatory system**. The artery taking de-oxygenated blood to the lungs is called the pulmonary artery. The pulmonary vein brings oxygenated blood back from the lungs, and enters the heart via the left atrium.

The systemic circulatory system

From the left atrium, oxygenated blood passes through the bicuspid valve into the left ventricle. It then passes through another semilunar valve and out through the aorta into the **systemic circulatory system**. The muscle in the left side of the heart is stronger because it has to pump the blood around the whole body.

Hints and Tips
Remember:
- *if it's going **away** from the heart, it starts with A (artery)*
- *if it's going towards the heart (that is, **visiting** the heart), it starts with a V (vein).*

To remember which:

- is the right side of the heart and which is the left, draw a face above the heart
- valve is on which side, the tri**cuspid** valve is on the **ri**ght side.

What happens to the blood when it visits the lungs?

When the de-oxygenated blood reaches the lungs, a process called gaseous exchange takes place. Carbon dioxide is removed from the blood and replaced with oxygen. This oxygenated blood is then taken back to the lungs via the pulmonary vein. A detailed analysis of this process is described on pages 32–4 under respiratory fitness (gaseous exchange).

There is a very important point to remember regarding the blood carried in the pulmonary artery and the pulmonary vein. These two vessels are exceptional in that in all other circumstances arteries carry oxygenated blood and veins carry de-oxygenated blood. However, the pulmonary artery carries de-oxygenated blood from the heart to the lungs. It is called the artery because it carries the blood *away*. Similarly, the pulmonary vein is called a vein because it carries blood *to* the heart, even though on this occasion it is oxygenated blood.

Test yourself

Cardiovascular fitness 1

1. Copy and complete this flow diagram of the heart using the words provided to label the diagram.

   Right ventricle   Left ventricle   Right atrium
   Left atrium   Septum   **5 marks**

2. Indicate with an arrow where the blood that is brought back from circulating around the body enters the heart and label it. **2 marks**

3. Indicate with an arrow the direction of the blood flow between the chambers of the heart and state the names of the two valves through which it flows. **2 marks**

4. Study the information in this topic, then set out the route through which the blood travels starting with the vena cava where it enters the heart on returning from the body. Set your answer out as a list. **12 marks**

5. When Jack had an operation it was discovered that he had a hole in his septum between the two atria. Explain the function of the septum and describe the problem this hole could have caused for him. **2 marks**

6. Describe why the functions of the pulmonary artery and pulmonary vein are unusual and unique in the way they work. **2 marks**

Total 25 marks

6 Cardiovascular fitness 2

For this topic you should study:
- blood vessels
- blood.

Having revised some aspects of the heart and looked at their importance in terms of how they relate to sporting performance, it is important to investigate the other two aspects of cardiovascular fitness – that is, the blood and the blood vessels.

The blood vessels

Arteries, veins and **capillaries** all carry blood, but they are different in construction.

Arteries have thick walls with no valves, and are more elastic than veins. They carry blood away from the heart and they pulsate as the heart beats. The blood they carry is oxygenated and is pumped at a high pressure. The aorta is the biggest and most powerful of the arteries, and takes blood from the left ventricle of the heart. Arteries that branch off from the aorta and transport blood to various organs are smaller. Arterioles branch off from arteries and are smaller still. All of these vessels carry oxygenated blood away from the heart.

Veins have thinner walls than arteries; they have valves and are less elastic. They carry de-oxygenated blood to the heart at lower pressure than arteries and rarely pulsate. Tiny capillaries provide the link between arteries and veins. Oxygenated blood from the arterioles enters the capillaries and delivers its oxygen and nutrients to the muscles and tissue. The capillaries then pick up waste products (including carbon dioxide), and this de-oxygenated blood is transported through the venules, veins, vena cava and back to the heart.

Aorta – Arteries – Arterioles – Capillaries – Venules – Veins – Vena Cava

Capillaries can carry both oxygenated and de-oxygenated blood.

Hints and Tips
Remember that the pulmonary artery and vein are exceptions to the rule.
- *The pulmonary artery carries de-oxygenated blood away from the heart to the lungs. It is called an artery because it carries blood away from the heart.*
- *The pulmonary vein carries oxygenated blood towards the heart from the lungs. It is called a vein because it carries blood to the heart.*

Blood

In some ways, the cardiovascular system could be compared with the London underground system. The network of tunnels through which the trains pass are the arteries, veins and capillaries; the trains are the blood and the people in the trains are what makes London work. Each passenger has a different job and is dropped off at a different place to carry out their work. At the end of the day when they have finished their jobs, they are picked up again and taken home to be replenished (food and sleep) before returning the next day to carry out their work again.

In the cardiovascular system the blood cells represent the passengers. These are carried in **blood plasma**, a pale straw-coloured liquid carrying glucose to the cells and waste products from them.

Within the blood cells there are **red cells**. These are coloured by a pigment called **haemoglobin**, which attracts oxygen from the lungs and delivers it to the tissues. There are also **white cells**, which are transparent. These are the cells that seek out and destroy any infections. Some of these kill off bacteria and viruses. Others combat what are known as pathogens.

The blood also contains **platelets**, which are cells that rush to the scene of the injury when we cut ourselves and help to stem the flow of blood by clotting and repairing the wound.

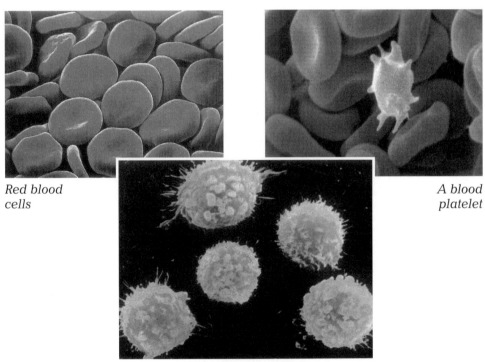

Red blood
cells

A blood
platelet

White blood cells

Hints and Tips

- *Red blood cells carry haemoglobin.*
- *Haemoglobin attracts oxygen.*
- *Blood plasma carries the blood cells.*

- *White blood cells fight infection.*
- *Platelets help to clot blood.*

Test yourself

> ## Cardiovascular fitness 2

1. Cardiovascular fitness is one of the most important areas of health-related exercise. Name the three components it involves.

   _____, _____, _____ _____   **3 marks**

2. The people whose profiles are given on pages 1 and 2 would all benefit from cardiovascular fitness training as it improves their ability to bring _____ blood back from the _____ first through the _____, which carry both _____ and _____ blood, then through the _____, then the _____ before it is finally returned to the _____ _____ of the heart through the _____ _____.   **9 marks**

3. The blood must travel from the heart to the _____ through the _____ artery, which is the only artery to carry _____ blood. Blood is brought back to the heart via the _____ _____, which is the only _____ to carry _____ blood.   **6 marks**

4. The pulmonary vein delivers blood to the heart via the top chamber, which is called the _____ _____ and passes through the _____ valve into the _____ _____ before entering the _____ having passed through another valve called the _____ valve.   **5 marks**

5. The vessels that carry blood have different requirements and the reasons can best be understood by considering what the heart of Garry (our elite young footballer) might be doing when he is playing hard:

   His muscles need glucose (energy) which is carried in _____ _____ in the arteries. The arteries will _____ as his heart beats, so that the blood will be pumped at _____ pressure. _____ is attracted by _____ that is carried in the _____ _____ _____ and this will provide the _____ his muscles need.

   Sometimes in a game, a hard tackle may result in an injury or cut. Should this happen, _____ in the blood will help with clotting, while the white cells carried in his blood will destroy any _____.   **9 marks**

   Total 32 marks

Section B: Training and exercise

7 How training and fitness affect the heart

For this topic you should study:
- how training and fitness affect the heart
- links between health, exercise and fitness
- how these factors affect performance.

Earlier in the revision programme, we revised definitions for health, exercise, fitness and performance. In the last few topics, we learned about the cardiovascular system. In this section, we will see how all these factors are connected and can be used, through training, to improve cardiovascular fitness, and how by doing this we can improve both health and performance.

Training is a very broad term. In this course, we are concerned with the physical aspects, not training to improve skill. The aim is to improve health and/or physical performance, defined as 'how well a task is completed'.

> **Definition**
> **Heart rate** (or pulse rate) is the number of times the heart beats per minute. It is not unusual for those last two words to be omitted in answers to questions in examinations – but this makes the answer incorrect. Heart rate is important in relation to fitness, exercise and training, as it is a good indicator of a person's fitness.

A low heart rate or pulse rate suggests a good standard of fitness.

Heart rate (pulse rate)

A trained athlete will usually have a low pulse rate. For example, an Olympic middle distance runner may have a pulse rate of 40 beats per minute (BPM) and, as we saw on page 21, Miguel Indurain, the Spanish cyclist, had a resting heart rate of 27 BPM.

An average pulse rate is about 72 beats per minute. This can be affected by a number of factors, including age, gender and body type. The pulse rate is usually higher in older people; women are more likely to have a higher pulse rate than men; bigger/fatter people are more likely to have a higher pulse rate than smaller or thinner people. This is an additional factor that can affect the performance of players who are overfat, in addition to reducing mobility, speed and endurance. Our posture can also affect our pulse rate. If we stand up it will rise; if we sit or lie down it will fall. When we eat, get emotionally aroused or angry, for example, our pulse rate will rise, and it can also be affected by our body temperature and our environment. A final factor that can affect heart rate, fitness and performance is smoking.

As stated earlier, heart rate or pulse rate can be affected by age. As we get older, our resting pulse rate usually increases and our maximum pulse rate reduces. As a result, we cannot work as hard or for as long when we get older – yet another factor affecting performance.

Maximum heart rate

There is a formula that can be used to work out a person's maximum heart rate (it is the same for women and men):

220 – age = maximum heart rate

So, for Luke who is 20, his maximum heart rate is:

220 – 20 = 200 BPM

Stroke volume

Definition
Stroke volume is the amount of blood pumped by the heart with each beat.

We can improve our stroke volume with training. As we get fitter our heart can pump more blood per beat and therefore does not need to beat so often. Also, when we exercise or compete (perform) regularly, the heart becomes capable of working more efficiently.

Cardiac output

Definition
Cardiac output is the amount of blood pumped by the heart each minute.

This is controlled by the heart rate (pulse rate) and the stroke volume, and can be expressed by the formula:

Cardiac output = heart rate × stroke volume

Hints and Tips
- *Be able to define heart rate, stroke volume and cardiac output.*
- *Understand the relationship between these three.*
- *Be able to explain how exercise and training can improve these factors.*
- *Understand and explain how this relates to improved performance.*

What does training do with regard to cardiovascular fitness?

Training enables the heart to pump more blood per beat. This means that more red blood cells are available to carry more haemoglobin, which enables more oxygen to be available for our muscles to work. At the same time, more carbon dioxide can be eliminated. Training increases the size of the heart muscle and also its thickness, strength and efficiency. This means we can work harder for longer periods of time, which enables us to perform better in endurance events such as running, swimming and cycling.

Testing cardiovascular fitness

There are a number of ways to test cardiovascular fitness level. Many of these are maximal tests, which test a person to exhaustion. Care must be taken when using them. You may have heard of the following tests:

- the bleep test
- Cooper's 12-minute run test
- the Harvard step test
- the PWC (physical work capacity) 170 test
- the 1.5-mile run test
- the maximum oxygen uptake test.

These tests can be used to test the fitness of a person before starting a fitness programme, or to re-test that person after he/she has trained using a set programme for a certain time to see whether there is any improvement in fitness.

Resting heart rate (pulse rate)

Resting heart rate, commonly known as pulse rate, is a good measure of our cardiovascular fitness level, so it is important to know what your resting pulse rate (RPR) is. A fit adult would normally have a RPR of 50 to 60 BPM. This person may not be training for performance at a high level, but simply for enjoyment and health. Although training and exercise are important to improve performance in cardiovascular activities (those that require good fitness of the heart, blood and blood vessels), it can also contribute to cardiovascular health.

Working pulse rate

We have looked at a way to find our maximum pulse rate and at the other extreme our resting pulse rate. It is also important to know what our pulse rate is when we are training (working) or exercising, and this is usually taken immediately after we stop running, swimming, cycling or whatever exercise we are doing.

Recovery rate

During exercise or immediately after we stop exercising, our pulse is at its working rate. Our recovery rate is the amount of time it takes for our pulse to return to its resting pulse rate. We would normally take the pulse at the end of each subsequent minute after we stop exercising until we reach our resting rate again. The recovery time is another excellent measure for testing fitness – the shorter the recovery rate, the higher the level of fitness.

Hints and Tips
Know what is meant by and how to apply:
- *resting pulse rate*
- *working pulse rate*
- *recovery rate.*

Test yourself

How training and fitness affect the heart

1. Heart rate is the number of times the heart beats. True or false?   **1 mark**

2. A fit athlete will have a low heart rate. True or false?   **1 mark**

3. There are a number of factors that can affect a person's pulse rate. Give three examples that will cause a person's pulse rate to be high.   **3 marks**

4. Albert is aged 92. Although he is fit for his age would you expect him to have a higher or lower maximum pulse rate than Jack, who is 56?   **1 mark**

5. Anita is 66 and Louise is 44. Work out the maximum heart rate for each of these women. Show your working method.   **3 marks**

6. Define the term stroke volume.   **1 mark**

7. What happens to our stroke volume as we get fitter?   **1 mark**

8. Cardiac output (CO) is connected to heart rate (HR) and stroke volume (SV) by a formula. Complete the formula: CO =   **1 mark**

9. After Louise gave up playing badminton, as well as putting on weight she lost a lot of cardiovascular fitness. Six months ago, she began to use her exercise bicycle regularly. Explain what will have happened to her cardiac output, stroke volume and heart rate during the last six months.   **3 marks**

10. Explain how Louise will be able to cope better with oxygen and carbon dioxide circulation now that she is fitter.   **2 marks**

11. When Louise decides to go for the occasional game of badminton with her husband, how will this fitness affect her performance?   **1 mark**

12. When Louise began her programme, her husband arranged for her to do a fitness test first. Give two reasons why he wanted her to have the test.   **2 marks**

13. When Louise does her bicycle training she uses her resting pulse rate, working pulse rate and recovery rate. Explain what each of these pulse rates are and what use they may be to Louise with regard to her fitness.   **5 marks**

Total 25 marks

8 Respiratory fitness

For this topic you should study:
- the parts of the respiratory system
- how the respiratory system works.

The respiratory system is not a part of the cardiovascular system, but it is closely associated with it and it is very important in relation to both health and performance.

Breathing

When we breathe in, the muscles between our ribs (**intercostal muscles**) contract. This causes the chest to expand both upwards and outwards. At the same time the **diaphragm** contracts, flattens and lowers, changing from a dome shape to a flat shape. The thorax (chest compartment) is lined with the pleural membrane, which in turn is stuck to the outside of the lungs. Therefore, when the ribs lift upwards and outwards, the lungs are also pulled outwards. As the pressure inside the lungs is reduced, air rushes in through the nose and mouth.

The passage of air

As air passes through the nose, it is filtered by the hairs, warmed by the blood vessels and moistened by water vapour before passing through a tube called the trachea. The wider area at the top of the trachea is the larynx (voice box). At the bottom, the trachea branches left and right into the **bronchi**, which take air to the left and right lungs respectively. The trachea and the bronchi also have microscopic hairs covered with mucus to ensure that the air is cleaned. The smaller **bronchioles** branch off the bronchi until at the very ends they reach tiny sacs called **alveoli**.

Alveoli

The linings of the alveoli are very thin. They must be moist and clean in order to work efficiently. If they are not, this will affect our performance in sporting activities because the effective exchange of gases (oxygen and carbon dioxide) required for this sporting performance does not take place. It will also affect our health and cause breathlessness with even minor exertion – for example, walking uphill. Smoking also affects the alveoli. The chemicals in smoke destroy the alveoli. This results in permanent 'holes' in the lower lungs, leaving the alveoli unable to perform their function. It could also lead to chronic lung diseases such as emphysema.

- *Bacteria and cold/flu viruses find perfect conditions in the lungs.*
- *Pollution affects the efficiency of the lungs.*
- *Smoking ruins your lungs.*

Hints and Tips
- *Learn how the respiratory system works.*
- *Understand how we breathe in and out.*
- *Be able to explain how the respiratory system affects health and performance.*

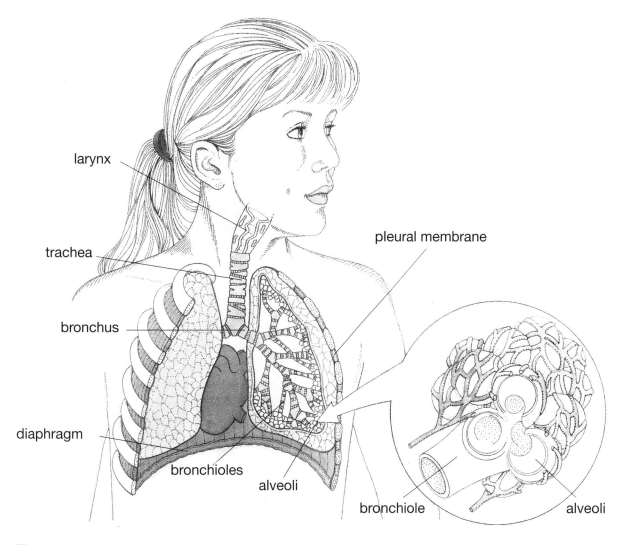

The respiratory system

Gaseous exchange

This is the point at which the cardiovascular system (the heart, blood and blood vessels) and the respiratory system meet. We saw on page 23 how the systemic circulatory system delivers oxygen to the muscles and picks up waste products. The pulmonary artery returns the blood to the lungs from the heart.

We saw on page 32 that oxygen-rich air (which carries at this point about 20% oxygen and 0.4% carbon dioxide) is delivered to the alveoli in the lungs. The alveoli come into very close contact with capillaries, and this is where gaseous exchange takes place. The capillaries contain red blood cells with haemoglobin which attracts oxygen. They also contain less oxygen (16%) and more carbon dioxide (4%) than the alveoli. This causes oxygen to be taken into the capillaries, and carbon dioxide is taken out. The oxygen picked up by the haemoglobin is delivered to the working muscles via the cardiovascular system (circulatory system) and gaseous exchange takes place again at the opposite end of the chain.

It is at this point that a series of chemical reactions takes place in order for the energy in the form of glucose and oxygen to be exchanged for carbon dioxide and water (tissue respiration). It is important to understand this:

Glucose + Oxygen → Energy + Carbon Dioxide + Water

Respiration and sport

Respiration is very important in endurance events, such as the Tour de France cycle race or the Olympic 5000 metres. Carbon dioxide and waste products are produced in high quantities in these events, and oxygen as well as glucose are needed to replenish the working muscles.

- *Tidal volume is the amount of air breathed in and out with each breath.*
- *Training can increase your tidal volume and the efficiency of your lungs.*
- *Vital capacity is the largest amount of air that can be breathed in and out of the lungs by the most forceful inspiration and expiration.*
- *It is a great advantage to endurance athletes to have a large vital capacity.*

Hints and Tips
- *Understand and be able to explain gaseous exchange and relate it to sporting situations.*
- *Understand and describe briefly the aspects of respiration.*

Test yourself

1. Complete the paragraph below, which describes the breathing process. Use each of the words and phrases listed in the tinted box at least once.

> pressure inside; intercostal muscles; flattens; upwards and outwards; lowers; breathe in; dome shape; diaphragm; air rushes in; contract

When we _____ _____ the _____ _____ _____ to start the process, causing our chest to expand both _____ _____ _____. At the same time the _____ contracts, _____ and _____ changing from a _____ _____ to a flat shape. The thorax (chest compartment) is lined with the pleural membrane, which in turn is stuck to the outside of the lungs. Therefore when the ribs lift _____ _____ _____ , the lungs are also pulled outwards. As the _____ _____ the lungs is reduced, _____ _____ _____ through the nose and mouth.　**10 marks**

2. Identify each of the five parts of the respiratory system labelled A–E on this diagram.　**5 marks**

3. Matt C and Jill do a lot of their training by running on the roads in London where heavy traffic pollutes the air. It helps, therefore, that before the air reaches their lungs it is cleaned, warmed and moistened. Explain this process and why it is so important in relation to the alveoli.　**4 marks**

4. During their training there is an increase in the exchange of gases (oxygen and carbon dioxide) that takes place in the lungs. During this exchange what percentage of each gas is given out and what percentage is taken in?　**2 marks**

5. The oxygen Matt C and Jill take in is delivered via the cardiovascular system to the working muscles where tissue respiration takes place. Complete the equation that expresses this.

Glucose + _____ → _____ + _____ _____ + _____　**2 marks**

6. The training that Matt C and Jill do increases the amount of air they can breathe with each normal breath, and also the amount they can breathe in and out with their most forceful breath. Explain the terms used to describe each of these.　**2 marks**

Total 25 marks

9 The effects of exercise

For this topic you should study:
- what happens to our bodies when we exercise or compete
- the link between these factors and our performance in competition or during exercise
- the effects of regular training and exercise
- the long-term benefits of exercise
- the role of aerobic and anaerobic activity in relation to exercise.

The immediate effects of exercise

When we exercise, especially cardiovascular exercise, there are several immediate effects on our bodies.

1. The heart will beat faster and stronger (as can be shown by a faster and stronger heart beat).

2. Breathing will quicken and deepen (we become breathless eventually).

3. Body temperature will rise.

4. We will start to sweat.

5. Our muscles will begin to ache (more blood is needed to be pumped around the body, so more waste products can be replaced with oxygen and glucose).

Faster heart rate

Heart rate is raised by the release of **adrenaline**. This is why heart rate can quicken in stressful situations when we are not necessarily exercising or performing. This rise in pulse rate enables more blood to be pumped to the lungs faster so that more oxygen can be circulated around the body. Training helps the body to cope better in these situations, as the heart of a fit person will be bigger and more used to working under such stress.

Quicker and deeper breathing

The harder we exercise or perform, the more frequently and the deeper we will breathe. An increase in breathing rate will help us to get more oxygen to the working muscles. However, if we work hard enough for long enough we will reach a point where we cannot get enough oxygen and our muscles will stop working. An example of this is when a person gets cramp and has to stop. Training will help us to overcome this, but there is a limit for everyone. A high red blood cell count, and therefore more haemoglobin, will result in an athlete or sports person being able to cope better with exercise, and sometimes drugs or illegal methods are used to improve a sports person's ability to cope in these situations (see 'Prohibited methods' and the text on EPO on page 83).

- *Training will help you to cope better with exercise.*
- *Training improves tidal volume.*
- *Training improves vital capacity.*

Rise in body temperature

When we exercise or perform our muscles generate heat. This, in turn, means body temperature rises above the normal range (between 36.4 and 37.2°C). We can regulate body temperature by sweating when we are too hot and shivering when we are too cold.

Sweating

Although most of the energy produced is used by the muscles, some of it is turned into heat and eventually we begin to sweat. This comes out of our pores and when sweat reaches the surface it evaporates. However, for it to evaporate it needs energy. It gets this from the body as heat, and as it uses this heat our temperature falls.

Two problems are caused by this action: the loss of water (as sweat), and the loss of salt with the sweat (which helps to prevent cramp). Both the water and the salt need to be replaced.

Water is the second most important body requirement after oxygen and it needs to be replenished or dehydration can occur. While playing sport we lose water, especially in games of long duration played in high temperatures. The event in which many competitors compete and in which dehydration is perhaps most evident is the marathon. This is always over two hours in duration and, for some people, over five hours. Water stations are provided for the runners. These runners are also encouraged to take on water before the start and in the early miles, because it is too late when they have been running for a long time.

Muscle ache

As we have seen, we need food to provide energy for our bodies to work, and this is carried in our blood in the form of glucose. We also need the oxygen that we get via the respiratory system, and this too is carried in our blood to the working muscles. Waste products such as carbon dioxide are exchanged via the blood. During exercise more glucose and oxygen are needed and more waste is produced. The heart beats faster until eventually the muscles cannot get enough oxygen, so a different method of getting energy is used which produces lactic acid. Eventually, if the lactic acid cannot be dispersed the muscle will ache. It may even cause cramp and the muscles will stop working. The athlete will have to rest until the blood can bring sufficient oxygen to the muscles. This is how it can affect performance.

Hints and Tips

- Know and be able to explain why a rise in body temperature, sweating and muscle ache happen as immediate effects of exercise.
- Be able to explain these effects for different games and activities.
- Be able to link these effects to what you know about the respiratory system.

Long-term benefits of exercise and training

Most team games need a combination of aerobic and anaerobic fitness, and therefore the training required for them will include a combination of both. Whichever form is emphasised, or if there is a combination of both, there will be certain long-term effects on the cardiovascular system, the heart, the blood and the blood vessels. These effects will have the following benefits.

- The risk of coronary heart disease (CHD) will be reduced.
- You will be able to work harder for longer.

Aerobic and anaerobic training and exercise

Training and exercise for cardiovascular fitness can be aerobic, anaerobic or a combination of both. Whatever method is used, effects such as the following will occur.

- The heart will pump more blood per beat (stroke volume).
- The heart will recover quicker (recovery rate).
- The heart will beat slower while resting (resting pulse rate).
- The number of capillaries will increase.
- The cardiovascular system will become more efficient (improve performance).

- *The production of energy with oxygen is called* **aerobic respiration**.
- *The production of energy without oxygen is called* **anaerobic respiration**.

Improved cardiovascular fitness will result in better performance in many sporting activities. **Aerobic fitness** will help in endurance events and games that go on over a long period of time – for example, swimming, squash, tennis, badminton, football, netball and rugby. **Anaerobic fitness** will help in the activities where shorter, faster bursts of energy are required – for example, sprint events up to 400 metres, the shorter races in swimming and any sprinting in the games already mentioned, where a combination of aerobic and anaerobic fitness is required.

Aerobic fitness helps athletes to train for long-distance events

Cardiovascular fitness and health

Throughout this section we have seen not only how cardiovascular fitness can help us to improve our fitness (and therefore our ability to perform better in our chosen sports) but also the many benefits it has on health.

It helps to:

- reduce blood pressure
- reduce stress
- burn off excess calories, improving our body composition
- motivate us not to smoke
- increase our heart in size, thickness and strength
- increase the size of the chambers of the heart.

Coronary heart disease (CHD) causes more deaths in the western world than any other disease, and smoking causes more deaths through heart attacks than it causes through cancer. However, there are many other reasons why people die from heart disease, including hereditary conditions and infections. Exercise can help to prevent most of these.

Aerobic training

Aerobics has grown into a massive fitness industry. This kind of training became popular more than twenty years ago and developed from what was known as 'exercise to music'. These days, not only can you take aerobic classes, but also there are books, television programmes and videos by famous personalities giving advice on this type of training. This kind of exercise includes step aerobics and water/aqua aerobics.

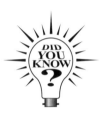

Aerobic fitness is the ability to exercise, compete or perform for a long time, at a level that allows the cardiovascular and respiratory systems to cope physiologically. The term 'aerobics' was invented by Dr Kenneth Cooper who also invented the Cooper's 12 Minute Run Test.

Hints and Tips
- *Understand and be able to explain the difference between aerobic and anaerobic exercise.*
- *Understand and be able to explain the effects of exercise and training, and the long-term benefits of cardiovascular fitness.*

Anaerobic training

Anaerobic exercise, training or performance can only last for a short period of time, normally up to about 40 seconds for a trained athlete, because of the high intensity of the exercise. Even then, many of these athletes will be seen gasping for breath at the end of their performance in order to get as much oxygen back into their respiratory system as possible, while at the same time eliminating as much waste as possible. In this way they are able to repay what is known as their **oxygen debt**, the amount of debt being the amount of oxygen used in the **recovery time** in excess of what they would normally have used had they been resting. In training to improve anaerobic fitness the person will need to have rests in order to recover enough to perform again at a high intensity.

Anaerobic fitness is the ability to work at a high intensity for a short period of time, and repay your respiratory system after completing the training session or performance.

Cross-training

Cross-training is a method of training that involves variety in order to take the boredom out of repeated daily training sessions. The different types of training would be designed to complement each other and would therefore include a mixture of activities for aerobic fitness. A typical programme might contain aerobics, swimming, using the rowing machine, brisk walking, jogging and step aerobics. These might take place on different days or the combination might form a complete training session. Cross-training might also include sessions for other forms of fitness such as weight training in order to gain all-round fitness.

Hints and Tips
- *Be able to explain how aerobic and anaerobic fitness affect performance in different activities.*
- *Be able to explain how oxygen debt affects performance and how its effects are repaid.*
- *An endurance athlete might experience oxygen debt in a long-distance race that ends in a sprint finish.*

Different sports require different amounts of aerobic and anaerobic fitness. A marathon is at the aerobic end of the spectrum, and the 100m sprint is at the anaerobic end.

A sprint finish often causes oxygen debt.

Test yourself

The effects of exercise

1. Jill (42) runs cross-country and recently competed for her club in the Ladies County Championship with over 300 runners. The course started at the bottom of a steep hill with a run of about 500 metres to the top before it flattened out. In the team talk before the race it was decided that it was important to reach the top of the hill in a good position. This meant a fast start. When Jill reached the top she was in about 30th position, but the immediate effects of the fast start were beginning to show. State what you think would be the first three of these effects and explain why they happen.   **6 marks**

2. Not only was the course hilly, but also it was very muddy. By the end of the race a lot of runners who were not as fit as Jill were beginning to show signs of tiredness and cramp. Explain what was building up in their muscles that would bring on cramp, and what was needed in the muscles to get rid of it.   **2 marks**

3. What is the name given to the condition these runners found themselves in?   **1 mark**

4. Jill has trained hard for over twenty years and has built up tremendous fitness brought about by both types of training used for cardiovascular fitness. What are these two types of training called?   **2 marks**

5. Explain with regard to oxygen what each term used to describe these forms of training means.   **2 marks**

6. At the end of the race Jill had to do a sprint finish to hold off a challenge from another runner. Which type of training would benefit her in this situation?   **1 mark**

7. Explain briefly the difference between the two types of training in your answer to question 4.   **2 marks**

8. Jill also plays netball. Which of these two types of training would be most suitable for netball and which most suitable for cross-country?   **2 marks**

9. Both of these training methods will bring about certain effects that will improve the performance of the cardiovascular system. Give three ways in which the cardiovascular system can be improved by training and briefly explain each of them.   **6 marks**

10. The training that Jill has done over the years will have a direct benefit to her health. Give one example of how she might benefit.   **1 mark**

Total 25 marks

10 The principles of training

For this topic you should study:

- the principles of training
- target zones and their use in exercise programmes
- plotting and evaluating training and recovery rates.

Systematic programming

Both aerobic and anaerobic training will improve cardiovascular fitness, but training to improve health or training to improve performance must be **systematic** if it is to achieve optimum success. The first few weeks of a new year are probably the most popular time for people to start a training programme, with the idea that they will lose the extra pounds put on after the Christmas festivities. However, without a systematic planned programme, they are likely to falter in achieving their targets.

Individual needs

We have seen under the section on cross-training (page 40) that there are many ways in which people can get fit. In order to get the most from a training programme the planning should take into account each person's **individual needs**. Individuals should consider the following points.

- What they want to achieve from their programme, and how to set their goals/targets accordingly.
- What level of fitness they want to reach and how they are going to reach to that level.
- What they like doing, when and where they can train, what facilities are available to them and at what cost.
- Whether they like training alone, with a partner or in a group.

When they have considered these points they can work out how they are going to achieve their targets. Although these points seem to target health and fitness they also apply to people who wish to train to achieve high performance in their various sports.

Specificity

Under this principle the training plan is designed to raise fitness to improve **specific performance**. This could simply be cardiovascular fitness, but it applies very much to the overall training programme to improve a person's whole performance in their chosen sport. For many years the training of Tiger Woods has included fitness, diet, skill and mental approach (he had a sports psychologist from the age of ten). All this training was specifically designed to make him a better golfer – and it did! In some sports specificity might apply to training for certain positions – for example, the backs in rugby, goalkeepers in football and hockey or shooters in netball.

The FITT principle

This principle has four aspects to it, each of which needs to be considered whatever the programme.

F is for **frequency**, or how often (how many times each week) you train. It should be a minimum of three times a week for health and fitness, but probably at least once every day if you want to win an Olympic gold medal.

I is for **intensity**, or how hard you train. For cardiovascular fitness there is a target range to gauge how hard you are working, and improvement will be dependent partly on this element. This will be dealt with in more detail under the overload principle that is dealt with next.

T is for **time**, or how long your training sessions last. A minimum of 20 minutes is recommended for general fitness, but it would be much longer than this at a higher level of sports training.

T is for the **type** of training you intend to do. This will depend on what you want from your training. We have seen that cardiovascular fitness can be gained from a wide variety of activities as long as the pulse rate is raised for a long enough period of time and to a high enough intensity.

Overload

The principle of **overload** is very much linked with the intensity aspect of the FITT principle (see above). In terms of cardiovascular fitness it is also linked to maximum heart rate, working heart rate and recovery time. Overload relates to thresholds of training and target zones (or target range). We learned earlier that you find your maximum heart rate as follows:

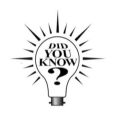

220 – age = maximum heart rate

In order to work out your target zone, calculate 80% and 60% of your maximum heart rate. The training intensity for professional sports people will be above the 80% training threshold, while a person starting out on a fitness programme would be working near to the 60% level. Once a reasonable level of fitness has been established you could work some sessions at a higher level of intensity in order to raise your level of fitness.

Overload does not mean too much training.

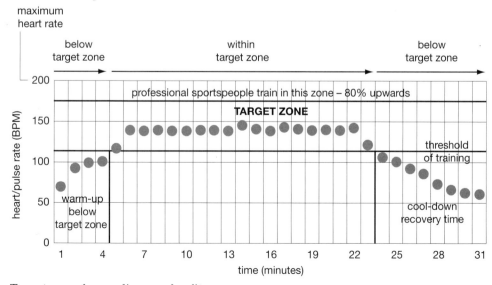

Target zone for cardiovascular fitness

Regularity and moderation

Training must take place regularly (**regularity**) if progress is to be made. We cannot train on Saturday and Sunday and then take five days off, otherwise we will improve and then slip back. However, if people burst into a very strenuous programme it could be unsafe and/or they might soon give up. Therefore, **moderation** should be considered when planning a **PEP**.

Progression

If training is to be successful it has to be planned and monitored over a period of time. In the most simple of PEPs this would be over an approximate timescale of six to eight weeks. The reason for monitoring a plan is to make sure that further improvement or **progression** takes place, and for this to happen it has to be evaluated after a set period of time, for example, every two or six weeks. As we have already seen, there are numerous ways for progress to be measured. Using various pulse rates, Cooper's 12 Minute Run Test or the Bleep Test are ways of evaluating a programme. Once the programme has been evaluated the next six-week programme can be planned showing progress (progression) from the first one. This too will be evaluated after a set period of time and so on. This progression can take many forms using the principles of training – for example, training for a longer period of time each session, training at a higher intensity, introducing new activities and so on. The following is an example of a six-week training programme.

- 2 sessions of 15 minutes for 2 weeks = 30 minutes total
- 2 sessions of 20 minutes for 2 weeks = 40 minutes total
- 3 sessions of 20 minutes for 2 weeks = 60 minutes total

Double the amount of training for the first two weeks shows progression. A slightly fitter performer might try the following.

- 3 sessions of 20 minutes for 3 weeks = 60 minutes total
- 4 sessions of 30 minutes for 3 weeks = 120 minutes total

This again actually doubles the amount of training and also takes into account **systematic programming**, **individual needs** and aspects of the **FITT principle** of training.

Reversibility

If training takes place in a planned and informed manner, applying the principles of training outlined above, then progress in fitness levels and therefore performance will take place over a long period of time. The opposite or reverse is also true. Less training, less intensity, missed training sessions, injury and illness are all causes of this final principle of **reversibility**.

Personal Exercise Programme (PEP)

A **Personal Exercise Programme** (PEP) can be planned to emphasise particular areas of health-related exercise, but most often it will include activities that help to develop all areas. The principles outlined earlier provide all the information required to build and monitor a PEP. They can be used specifically or for a general fitness programme. It will help to produce a plan designed for a student's specialist activity – for example, football, netball or swimming. It should include all aspects of fitness required for the particular activity and could include many of the various ways of monitoring progress demonstrated here.

Warm-up

The exercise or training session is made up of three distinct parts: the **warm-up**, the **main activity** and the **cool down**. There are three reasons to warm-up.

1. To prevent injury.

2. To improve performance.

3. To prepare psychologically.

Sports people often use specialist warm-ups tailored to their specific sports. Even so, a warm-up should start with gentle cardiovascular exercise to raise the pulse rate (heart rate) gradually. This kind of exercise will include jogging, cycling, easy swimming or a similar activity. The time spent will depend on the person, level of fitness, event or intensity of the activity. This should be followed by a series of exercises appropriate to the activity – for example, a shot putter might do different exercises to a racing cyclist. These exercises should be static, held for about 10 to 15 seconds and cover a full range for the activity, usually starting at the top of the body and working downwards, finishing just before the main activity.

Main activity

The main activity could be a physical training session – running, cycling, swimming, aerobics – or it might be a skills session to improve performance in, say, football, netball or table tennis. It could even be a training session followed by a skills session.

Cool down

The cool down is a very important part of the exercise session, although it is often neglected. It should follow a similar pattern to the warm-up, gradually returning the pulse rate to normal and allowing the muscles to be stretched to prevent stiffness and soreness by dispersing lactic acid. Stretches in the cool down should last longer than in the warm-up – about 30-5 seconds.

Hints and Tips
- *Understand and be able to explain how to plan a PEP using the principles of training.*
- *Understand and be able to explain an exercise session including the warm-up, main activity and cool down.*

Test yourself

The principles of training

Barrie has just turned 50. He played football for his local club for twenty years before retiring from the game aged 38. Knowing how important exercise and fitness are to health he trains regularly six times a week, running four times over the same three-mile course (22 to 23 minutes, in the same direction) and cycling his mountain bike twice a week (25 minutes) over a five-mile course. He does a warm-up before and a cool down after each exercise session. He never runs on a Sunday because this is always his rest day.

1. Although knowing nothing about the principles of training, Barrie has managed to apply systematic programming to his training plan. Explain what is meant by systematic programming and why it is important.   **2 marks**

2. The programme that Barrie has planned suits his individual needs. Give at least three factors from the information above that show this principle fits his programme.   **3 marks**

3. Barrie still includes a number of aspects of training from his football days – for example, running backwards. When certain aspects such as this are included, which principle is being applied?   **1 mark**

4. From the information above, take each aspect of the FITT principle and explain how or if it is applied in Barrie's programme.   **4 marks**

5. Barrie may apply the overload principle, but he does not know what it is. Explain this principle using the terms 'thresholds of training' and 'target zone'.   **3 marks**

6. Barrie is interested in learning about the overload principle. Explain and find his target range for cardiovascular fitness.   **3 marks**

7. Without really knowing much about the principles of training, Barrie has actually put together quite a well-planned PEP. There is, however, one big gap – that is the principle that would answer his question: 'Why is it that I reached a certain point of fitness and have never improved from there?' Name this principle.   **1 mark**

8. Explain for Barrie how the principle in question 7 works within a PEP, naming three ways that could be used to monitor and evaluate his performance level.   **3 marks**

9. If you were to evaluate Barrie's PEP for six weeks, suggest one way in which he might change his programme in order to try to improve his fitness.   **1 mark**

10. In his training sessions, Barrie keeps strictly to the three parts of the exercise session. What are these three parts?   **3 marks**

11. Barrie is due to go into hospital for a cartilage operation. Which principle of training is likely to come into effect after this?   **1 mark**

Total 25 marks

11 Methods of training

For this topic you should study:
- interval training
- continuous training
- Fartlek training
- circuit training
- aerobic and anaerobic training.

There are many different ways in which we can train in order to improve cardiovascular fitness.

Interval training

> **Definition**
> **Interval training** includes periods of work followed by periods of rest. It includes work of high intensity and is good for anaerobic fitness.

This a method of training used by many top athletes in many types of sports – for example, team games such as football, netball, hockey and rugby; racket games such as tennis and squash; and individual sports such as swimming and athletics.

Interval training for team games
If you play team games such as those mentioned above and have trained with your school team or club outside of school, you may have been split into teams for training and then competed in shuttle relays of some kind. This is interval training.

Interval training for racket games
In racket games you may have been required to run shuttles – for example, to retrieve a shot from the forehand court, then run quickly to retrieve a shot from the backhand court for ten successive forehands and backhands. This is interval training.

Interval training for individual sports
In swimming you may have been required to start a two-length swim when the pool clock is at the top of the minute, then start another two-length swim when it reaches the top of the minute again. The quicker you swim your two lengths, the longer the rest you get. This is interval training.

Hints and Tips
Make sure you know about interval training for one of the activities you took for your practical so that you can give an example if required to do so in an examination.

Continuous training

Definition
Continuous training is working continuously at a moderate to slow pace.

Continuous training is used by many people in sports and is the most popular
training method. It is the type of training that competitive or professional sports
people might use before their season starts, usually called pre-season training.
The most common form of continuous training is running, normally referred to
as 'jogging'. It can also be cycling, rowing, brisk walking, swimming and
various forms of aerobics. In jogging terms, it is sometimes referred to as LSD
(Long, Slow, Distance), and it is a common way of training for people who run
in the London Marathon.

Fartlek training

Definition
Fartlek, Swedish for 'speedplay', involves running at various speeds over
varying distances and terrain.

Using the FITT principle, Fartlek training includes changes in intensity as in
hill running (up and down), sprinting over short and/or long distances, on sand,
through forest and in parks. It obtains similar effects to interval training in
improving aerobic and especially anaerobic fitness.

Circuit training

Definition
Circuit training combines a variety of exercises in a circuit. Participants move
on to another exercise after completing one successfully.

Circuit training is designed to improve cardiovascular fitness and muscular
endurance. The circuit is arranged in a series of stations so that one set of
muscles is exercised. Then these muscles are rested while another set is
exercised. In this respect, it resembles interval training. The exercises could be
done for a set number of repetitions or a set time; they could be the same number
of repetitions for each person or each person could work to his/her own schedule.
The session could have a wide variety of athletes taking part, but all working
towards their own specific goals – for example, triple jumpers, javelin throwers
and sprinters could work out together, but to their own specific programmes.

Hints and Tips
*Learn and remember to link the points covered above with other areas of the course.
For example, in circuit training the individually planned circuits satisfy the principles
of training regarding individual needs and systematic programming, and also the
FITT principles of specificity and intensity.*

Training sessions

Training sessions for cardiovascular fitness (and other areas of fitness) will vary for many reasons. These include the level of fitness of the athlete and the time of year – for example, pre-season as compared to the competitive season. The reasons for training will also have an influence on the type of training undertaken – that is, a competitive athlete will have a different training programme to a fitness seeker.

The aerobic training session

In terms of training, we have already considered the principle of overload and studied how to calculate the target zone for cardiovascular fitness training. So, for example, the cardiovascular fitness training range for a fifteen year-old would be 220–15 × 60%, and × 80% – in other words, it would be between 123 and 164 BPM. An aerobic training session that would enable this to take place in quite a controlled situation would be some form of low intensity, continuous training such as jogging or swimming. This would allow the pulse to work at a reasonably stable rate within a target zone. The graph for Matt C for such a session is set out below. Pulse rates were taken at rest, then at one-minute intervals for eight minutes of a training session. Pulse rates are shown on the vertical axis and time is shown on the horizontal axis.

The lower the intensity of your workout, the lower your pulse rate will be, but the pulse rate will stay fairly constant.

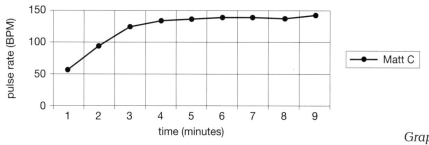

Graph 1

The anaerobic training session

By comparison, an interval training session would improve anaerobic fitness and would include work of high intensity – for example, sprints over, say, 60 to 80 metres or perhaps longer. This would raise the pulse rate to the higher end of the target zone. For the trained athletes for whom these sessions are designed they might be higher than the 80% we have used in our target zones. This is likely to produce a graph similar to the one shown below for Matt C.

The higher the intensity of your workout, the higher your pulse rate will be, but the pulse rate will decrease during the rest period.

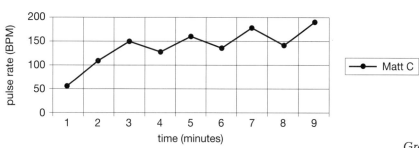

Graph 2

Test yourself

Methods of training

There are many different methods that we can use to improve fitness, but the one that you choose for yourself will depend on your reasons for taking part in sport or physical activity.

Insert the appropriate words in the spaces below to suit the person's profile. Some words are added at the start to give you an idea of what is required. The example words are in italics and underlined.

Where an answer requires repetition, the mark will only be given once.

1. Albert is 92 and runs in the London Marathon every year. His training consists of a *continuous* training programme that is mostly *jogging*, but could also include _____, _____ or _____. A graph shape of his working pulse rate during a jogging session closely resembles that shown in Graph 1 (page 49), but at 92 his _____ _____ would be between _____ and _____ BPM. This type of training would improve his _____ fitness.   **7 marks**

2. Matt C represents his county at the All England Schools Athletics Championships in the 400 metres, so he needs to improve his _____ fitness. In order to do this he uses _____ training. A graph of his working pulse rate using this method is shown in Graph 2 (page 49). The shape of this graph indicates that this type of training includes periods of _____ at a high _____ followed by periods of _____.   **5 marks**

3. Another type of training that might produce a similar shape graph is called _____. That means _____. This type of training can involve hill running, which will again increase the _____ and so raise the pulse rate higher.   **3 marks**

4. Luke is a national under-twenty throwing champion, so he does not use this type of training. However, in his winter training programme he uses _____ training for general fitness and muscular _____. This is very useful for him because it is not only _____ (which helps because he is living on a student grant), but also he can work with his friends who may be of _____ abilities, although their programme will suit their _____ needs. In this type of training, the exercises are arranged so that they suit the particular athlete and therefore fulfil the principle of specificity.   **5 marks**

5. Finally there is Garry, the YTS footballer. He needs a combination of the two types of fitness, so in his training programme he will include both. Other sports that require a similar combination of fitness include:

   Team game:_____ Racket game:_____ Other activity:_____   **3 marks**

                                                                        Total 23 marks

12 Muscular strength and muscular endurance

For this topic you should study:
- muscular strength
- isotonic contractions
- isometric contractions.

As we have already seen, cardiovascular fitness is the fitness of the heart, blood and the blood vessels. However, there are other aspects of fitness that can be improved with training. The training must be appropriate and planned for whatever aspect of fitness we are trying to improve.

Muscular strength

Definition
Muscular strength is the ability of the muscles to exert force, or the amount of force required to produce a single maximum effort. Weight lifting is a very good example of this.

In order to improve muscular strength it is necessary to lift heavy weights. If they are heavy we will not be able to lift them for many repetitions. We could work on what is known as the pyramid system; using a heavy weight we might do a set of five repetitions, followed by a set of four, then three, then two, then one. The starting weight would have been predetermined by finding our maximum for five repetitions commonly known as our five rep max.

Muscular endurance

Definition
Muscular endurance is the ability to use the voluntary (or skeletal) muscles (those attached to our skeleton that help us move) many times without getting tired.

In order to improve this type of strength it is necessary to do special training. This may take the form of exercises such as press-ups or sit-ups. However, if we take the weight training example again, we would have to lift lighter weights but do more repetitions, say ten reps, twenty or even thirty depending on what we are trying to achieve. These two aspects of strength are not totally separate from each other because improvement in one will lead to improvement in the other. We must plan our training to get the best effect.

Improved strength will:
- *increase your ability to work*
- *reduce the risk of injury*
- *help to prevent lower back pain*
- *improve your posture*
- *improve how you play your sport*
- *perhaps help to save your life (or someone else's)*
- *help you to recover from illness or injury.*

Hints and Tips
Remember that the same principles of training apply to both strength training and cardiovascular fitness.

Different ways that muscles contract

When muscles work they are said to contract. They can contract in different ways – for example they can contract and cause movement to take place, but they can also contract when no movement takes place. These two different ways of contracting need to be learned.

Isotonic contraction

> **Definition**
> An **isotonic muscle contraction** means that the muscle has contracted and movement has taken place.

This is what we would normally expect when we play sport, train or take part in anything physical. Examples include any shooting action in netball or basketball, a shot using a racket or bat, or an athletic movement in gymnastics, trampoline or dance.

For movement to take place muscles must contract.

Isometric contraction

> **Definition**
> When a muscle contracts but no movement takes place it is called an **isometric contraction**.

There are comparatively few examples of isometric contractions in sporting and training situations compared to the many examples of isotonic contractions. Holding a handstand in gymnastics is one example, or when one team is holding the other and no movement is taking place in a tug-of-war. In arm wrestling there is also often a point where neither protagonist can force the other into a losing position. An example in a team game would be in rugby, when one pack holds the other static.

When muscles contract they pull. Muscles cannot push.

Test yourself

Muscular strength and muscular endurance

Remember, you can look back to the profiles on pages 1 and 2 for more detail.

1. Luke, a junior throwing champion, works very hard to improve his technique and also areas of health-related exercise (HRE). For him, the most important of these is _____ _____, which can be defined as the _____ of the _____ to exert _____.   **2 marks**

2. One way for Luke to improve this area of fitness would be to do weight training using _____ weights and _____ repetitions.   **2 marks**

3. Jack, who is on a rehabilitation programme, will use weights to improve his _____ _____, which can be defined as the _____ to use the _____ muscles many times without getting _____.   **2 marks**

4. In order to improve in this area, Jack will be lifting _____ weights, but with _____ repetitions.   **2 marks**

5. Both Luke and Jack will be improving the strength of their _____ muscles, which are also known as the _____ muscles.   **2 marks**

6. Although the strength of these two people will improve, it will also help their ability in other areas. Three examples of these are: _____ _____ _____.   **3 marks**

7. When Luke and Jack are doing their strength or resistance training their muscles must _____ in order to work. When they do this but no movement takes place it is said to be an _____ contraction. Two examples in sport might be: _____ and _____. When movement takes place it is known as an _____ contraction.   **5 marks**

8. Two important points to remember about muscles are that they can _____ but they cannot _____.   **2 marks**

Total 20 marks

Section C: Anatomy and physiology

13 Bones

For this topic you should study:
- bones, and what they do
- bones and performance
- how bones are made.

Bones play a vital role in terms of how they can affect both participation and performance in sport.

Bones and performance

Bones form the structure of our frame or skeleton. The size of our bones affects our body build, our somatotype and our optimum body weight. Therefore they can affect the sports we may be best suited to.

Bones and blood

Red blood cells are important because the haemoglobin that makes them red carries oxygen around the body. Haemoglobin is made from red **bone marrow**. Because it carries oxygen, **haemoglobin** is very important in terms of cardiovascular fitness and can be improved by training.

The bones form the framework of our body, giving the body its shape and allowing us to stand upright. The lower part of the skeleton (appendicular skeleton) gives us stability, while the upper part (axial skeleton) gives us mobility in order to carry out many sporting actions. Bones are also important in terms of muscular strength in that they form an attachment for our muscles.

Finally, the bones of our skeleton protect vital organs. When a bone gets broken, although it can mend, our movement may be affected and in some cases can mean the end of a sports career for some people.

Hints and Tips
Make sure you can apply your knowledge about bones to other parts of the course – for example, diet and safety:
- *our diet should include sufficient amounts of calcium, a mineral that is vital for healthy bones and that can be found in dairy products such as milk, cheese and yoghurt*
- *with age, bone density decreases and our skeleton can become weak and fragile. This can result in a condition called osteoporosis, in which the bones break easily.*

Types of bones

Bones are classified into different types according to their function.

- Bones that protect are called **flat** or **plate bones**. Irregular bones such as the vertebrae in the spine also protect.
- Bones that act as levers are called **long bones**.
- The carpals in the wrist and the tarsals in the feet are called **short bones**.

It's easier to remember the bones if you chunk them into three blocks and remember them. Start at the top and work downwards from the cranium

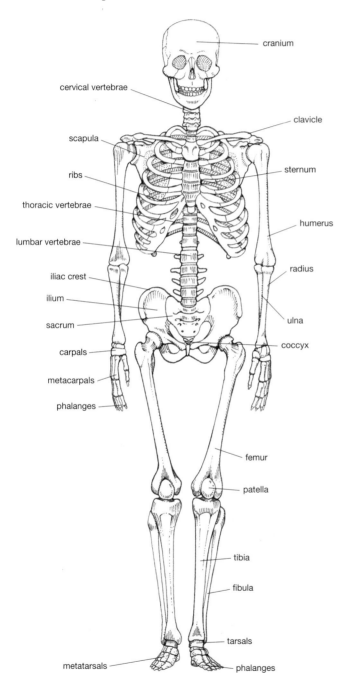

cranium
cervical vertebrae
scapula
clavicle
ribs
sternum
thoracic vertebrae
humerus
lumbar vertebrae
radius
iliac crest
ilium
ulna
sacrum
coccyx
carpals
metacarpals
phalanges
femur
patella
tibia
fibula
tarsals
metatarsals
phalanges

The human skeleton

Remembering 20 bones

Head and upper body = 7
Cranium
Clavicle
Ribs
And Sternum
Ilium
Sacrum

Arms and hands = 6
Humerus
Radius
And Ulna
Carpals
Metacarpals
And Phalanges

Legs and feet = 7
Femur
Patella
Tibia
Fibula
Tarsals
Metatarsals
And Phalanges

Bones of the upper body

Clavicle (collarbone): this is for protection, therefore known as a flat bone. It can often get broken in sporting situations.

Scapula (shoulder blade): this is for protection, and is also a flat bone.

Humerus, radius and **ulna**: the humerus is the bone in the upper arm. The radius and ulna are found in the lower arm, the **u**lna being the one **u**nderneath the arm. As they are used as levers, they are known as long bones.

Carpals: the short bones of the wrist. The long bones (because they are used as levers) in the hand and the fingers are called the **metacarpals** and **phalanges** respectively.

Bones of the lower body

Pelvis: this is formed by a combination of bones – the **ilium** (hip bone), the **pubis**, the **sacrum** and the **coccyx**. The latter two also form the bottom of the **vertebral column**, or spine.

In some ways the bones in the legs match the bones in the arms. The **femur** (which runs from the hip to the knee), the **tibia** (shin bone) and the **fibula** (found on the outside of the leg), are all long bones. The **patella** (kneecap) is a flat bone because it is involved with protection.

In the feet the **tarsals** (equal to the carpals in the wrist) are short bones, while the **metatarsals** and phalanges (same name as the phalanges in the fingers) are long bones.

Bones of the spine

We have learned about two of our vital organs, the heart and lungs. These are positioned in the chest and are protected by the ribs and sternum (breastbone). These bones are attached to the vertebral column (spine), which is made up of 33 irregular bones called **vertebrae**. The vertebrae are irregular bones that protect the spinal cord. They are divided into regions, known as the 'regions of the spine'. It might help to remember these in the following way.

- C1 to C7 are the **cervical** vertebrae.
- T1 to T12 are the **thoracic** vertebrae.
- L1 to L5 are the **lumbar** vertebrae.

Between each of the vertebrae is a very delicate disc that helps to absorb shock. The discs can slip out of place. When this happens it can be a very painful condition. The remaining two parts of the spinal column are known as the **sacrum** and the **coccyx**, which form a part of the pelvis.

Hints and Tips
- *Learn to use the correct names for the bones.*
- *Know that flat bones protect and long bones act as levers.*
- *Learn the names and positions of the regions of the spine.*
- *Make up a mnemonic to help you.*

How bones are made

All bones begin to form from **cartilage** before we are born. They gradually harden through the addition of calcium and other minerals, and grow upwards, downwards and around the central marrow cavity. This process is known as **ossification**.

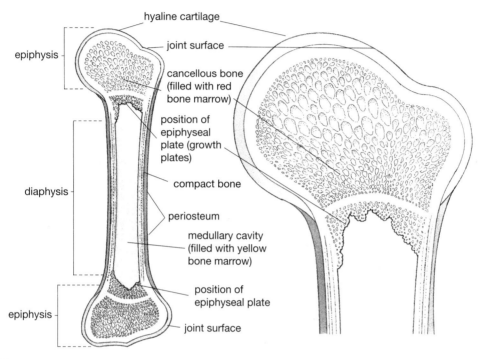

Bones

Epiphysis is the name for the end of a long bone.

Diaphysis is the name for the shaft of a long bone.

Periosteum is the tough membrane that surrounds the bone.

Compact bone is beneath the periosteum and forms the shaft of a long bone.

Cancellous bone is the spongy substance found inside the compact bone.

Hints and Tips
You can look after your bones by:
* *eating a well-balanced diet with sufficient calcium*
* *exercising*
* *not smoking.*

Test yourself

Bones

Remember, you can look back at the profiles on pages 1 and 2 for more detail.

1. The bigger our bones, the bigger our frame size. At 6 feet 5 inches it is not surprising that Luke, our twenty year-old national throwing champion is by far the biggest of our profiled people. We would therefore expect him to have the biggest bone _____ because this can affect the sports we choose and are good at. It can affect our _____ body weight, body build and therefore our _____ .

3 marks

2. Bones are important to all sports people, including those who need good cardiovascular fitness, because they need a good supply of haemoglobin, which is carried in the red _____ _____ , and which is made from red _____ _____ .

2 marks

3. Bones also _____ the two _____ , organs that are involved with our cardio-respiratory system. Apart from this, bones are important for all our profiled people for four additional reasons: _____

_____

_____ .

6 marks

4. Anita is 66, and she swims and line dances to keep herself fit and healthy. Of these two activities _____ _____ is the best for her bone health because _____ _____ activities are best for preventing the condition called _____ .

3 marks

5. Anita can also help to prevent the onset of this condition by making sure that in her _____ she has sufficient _____ , which is a _____ found in such products as _____ , _____ and _____ .

6 marks

6. Teresa, our 50 year-old grandmother, has a new grandson called Anthony. At his young age bones and diet are very important. Before he was born his bones were beginning to form from _____ , which was hardening. At this age children's bones grow _____ , _____ and _____ . This process is called _____ .

5 marks

7. In a long bone the end is called the _____ and the diaphysis is the name given to the _____ . The bones are covered by a tough membrane known as the _____ .

3 marks

Total 28 marks

Test yourself further

Bones

1. When Luke first joined the national throwing squad the coach had various tests done for him. One of these was to find out more about his body build. This entailed taking a fat measurement just below the shoulder blade, the clinical name for which is the _____. It is a _____ bone as it is used for _____.   **3 marks**

2. Bones are often injured in sporting situations, either broken or fractured. One of the most common of these breaks can happen to the collarbone, for which the clinical name is the _____. If this bone gets broken it can be recognised by the pain, irregularity at the site of the injury and also because the injured person wants to hold his/her lower arm across the waist.   **1 mark**

3. Another group of bones are called the _____ _____. They are all used as levers. There are three of these in the arm. The upper arm bone is called the _____ and the lower arm has two bones. The one that is underneath is called the _____ and the other is called the _____.   **4 marks**

4. There are two bones used as levers in the hand and fingers. The one in the hand is the _____, while the bones in the fingers (and also the toes) are called the _____. The bone in the wrist is a short bone called the _____.   **3 marks**

5. The main bone in the leg, the largest bone in the body, is called the _____. The bone below the knee is the _____, often called the shin bone, which has to be well protected in some sports because of the risk of injury, and the other on the outside is the _____. Finally there is the kneecap, or _____, which is a bone for protection.   **4 marks**

6. The ribs and sternum are found in the chest, and these protect the _____ and _____.   **1 mark**

7. Our spine is made up of 33 very special bones that are an _____ shape and are used for protection of the _____ _____. They are broken down into regions, starting at the top with the five bones of the _____ region, then the twelve bones in the _____ region and the _____ bones in the _____ region. The remaining two parts are the _____ and the _____, which form part of the _____.   **9 marks**

Total 25 marks

14 Joints

For this topic you should study:
- the definition of a joint
- types of joint
- movement possibilities
- synovial joints.

Definition
A **joint** is a place where two or more bones meet. The bones of our bodies are joined together to allow us to make certain movements possible.

Synovial joints

A **synovial joint** is strong, works smoothly, without any pain and gives adequate movement possibilities. The construction is quite complicated. In order to stop bones rubbing against each other, they are covered at the ends with **hyaline cartilage** (surrounded by **synovial fluid**), which is elastic and which cushions and protects the ends of the bones involved in the joint movement. The joint is surrounded by the **joint capsule**. Inside is the **synovial membrane**, which produces the synovial fluid that both protects and lubricates the joint. The knee is an example of a synovial joint.

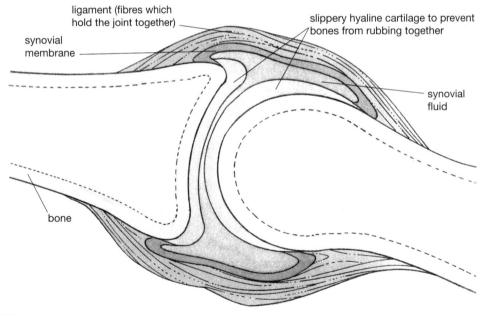

The knee joint

The shoulder and hip joints

The humerus in the arm and the femur in the leg each have a ball shape at the top of them that fits into a socket in the shape of a cup; they are ball and socket joints. The movement possibilities at these joints are similar, but the freedom of movement in the shoulder is far greater than in the hip.

In GCSE Physical Education we are concerned with five different types of movement:

- flexion
- extension
- adduction
- abduction
- rotation.

The shoulder allows all of these movements to take place, and although the hip allows the same movements the amount of movement is much more restricted. Flexion is an action that closes the angle made at a joint, while extension is the opposite. Abduction could be demonstrated by taking the arm away from the body sideways, while adduction is the opposite. Rotation is possible at the shoulder (and to a much lesser degree at the hip) by rotating the arm in its socket.

The knee and elbow joints

The knee and the elbow are both hinge joints, so they have no ball and socket connection. The knee in particular is a very complicated synovial joint. The joint is made between the femur and the tibia with the two smooth surfaces of these bones being held together by two very strong cruciate ligaments that cross (hence the name) inside the joint. An injury to these ligaments often signals the end of a sports person's career.

The hinge joint at the elbow is between the humerus and the ulna. The joint between the ulna and the radius is a pivot joint.

You should learn the movement possibilities that can take place for both the knee and the elbow joints.

Knee joint

- Flexion – the knee bends, decreasing the angle between the femur and the tibia to enable us to walk or run.
- Extension – the knee straightens, increasing the angle between the femur and the tibia to enable us to reach and stride.
- Rotation – a slight rotation is possible.

Elbow joint

- Flexion – the elbow bends, decreasing the angle between the humerus and the ulna when preparing to throw.
- Extension – the elbow straightens, increasing the angle between the humerus and the ulna to enable us to throw.
- Rotation – rotation is possible at the joint between the radius and ulna.

The wrist joint and joints of the fingers

The wrist and fingers provide a very complex set of joints that involves the carpals, metacarpals and the phalanges. A hinge action allows flexion, extension, adduction, abduction and rotation. This allows us to create complex spin actions, for example in cricket.

The ankle joint

The ankle joint is another hinge joint allowing flexion (know as dorsiflexion) and extension (known as plantaflexion). We can also turn our foot inwards (inversion) or outwards (eversion).

The sacroiliac joint

The sacroiliac joint is a synovial joint that works in a similar way to a hinge joint but also allows us slight rotation in our lower back. It is found between the sacrum and the hip.

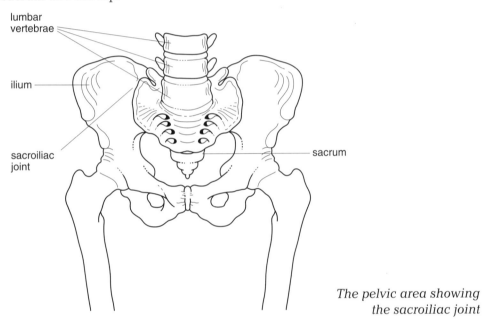

The pelvic area showing the sacroiliac joint

Cartilaginous joints

This type of joint is found in the spine, which has cartilage (discs) in between the hard surfaces. Unlike the synovial joint this joint does not have a synovial membrane. In the vertebral column we have free movement in the neck, where C1, the first cervical vertebrae, is known as the atlas and C2, the second vertebrae, is called the axis. These two form what is known as a pivot joint, which allows us to rotate our neck. Lower down the spine we have less movement but we can bend forward (flexion) and lean backwards (extension).

Hints and Tips
- *Learn the parts and the construction of a synovial joint.*
- *Know the different types of joints.*
- *Know about the types of movement possible at each type of joint.*
- *Be able to give examples from sport of different types of movement controlled by joints.*

Test yourself

> **Joints**

1. Joints are found in many places in the body where _____
   bones meet.   **1 mark**

2. Use any of the words from the box below to complete the following sentence
   on joints. You may use each word once, more than once or not at all.

   lubricates; synovial membrane; cushions; hinge; hyaline cartilage; disc;
   synovial fluid; protects; vertebrae; joint capsule; rubbing; elastic

   The knee is an example of a synovial joint that has _____ _____
   at the ends of the bones forming the joint. This is an _____
   substance which _____ the ends of the bones from _____
   together. Inside the _____ _____ is the _____
   _____ which produces _____ _____ that protects
   and _____ the joint.   **8 marks**

3. The joints at the hip and the shoulder are known as _____ ____
   _____ joints, and are used by most sports people both in training
   and competing. Swimming is a good example of a sport in which both the arms
   and legs work together. When Audrey swam competitively, one of her
   best events was butterfly, which uses both of these joints at the same time.
   The arm action in this stroke is a good example of the movement known as
   _____, the up movement (backwards) of the legs is an example
   of _____ and the down beat (forward) is a good example of the
   movement known as _____.   **4 marks**

4. The elbow and knee joints are both known as _____ joints. In
   breaststroke, the arms bend as you pull towards your body. This movement
   action at the elbow is known as _____. In breaststroke leg action, you
   straighten your knees when driving your legs backwards for propulsion. This
   action at the knee is known as _____. At the same time you extend
   your toes. This is called _____ flexion. By contrast as you recover
   your legs before the kick your feet will bend towards the tibia. This is called
   _____ flexion.   **5 marks**

5. When analysing Audrey's back crawl stroke it is possible to see that she
   _____ the joint at the elbow between the radius and the ulna in
   order to allow her to enter her little finger into the water first. She will
   _____ her fingers slightly towards her wrist and close them together,
   which is known as _____. At the start of the back crawl race she will
   take hold of the starting block and bend her spine forwards. This action of
   the spine is called _____. At the sound of the starter's hooter she
   will drive her feet against the wall and the action of the spine here is known as
   _____. At the finish of the race a novice swimmer who turns his/her
   head around to look for the finish wall will perform an action called rotation,
   which will take place between C1 and C2 vertebrae called the _____
   and the _____.   **7 marks**

   Total 25 marks

15 Muscles

For this topic you should study:
- the three different types of muscle tissue
- ligaments
- tendons
- cartilage.

Types of muscle tissue

There are three types of muscle tissue: **voluntary** (skeletal), **involuntary** (smooth) and **cardiac**.

We have already come across two of them, first when investigating cardiovascular fitness, and then when looking at training for muscular endurance and muscular strength.

> **Definition**
> Voluntary muscles are those muscles over which we have control. (They are also known as skeletal muscles because they are attached to the skeleton.) Involuntary muscles are those muscles over which we have *no* control. (They are also known as smooth muscles.)

Voluntary muscles
Voluntary muscle tissue is made up of **cylindrical fibres** and contributes a high percentage of our total weight. Improving muscular strength and muscular endurance are both about improving the strength of the voluntary muscles. We have already seen that for movement to take place at a joint a muscle must contract. We have also seen that muscles can pull but they cannot push. Therefore, in order to bend and straighten a joint, voluntary muscles work in pairs – one contracts while the other relaxes.

Involuntary muscles
Involuntary muscle tissue is made up of **spindle-shaped fibres**. These muscles are found in the digestive system and the urinary system.

Cardiac muscle
Cardiovascular fitness is about the fitness of the heart. The heart is a muscular pump. The heart wall muscle is known as cardiac muscle. Cardiac muscle is a type of involuntary muscle and the heart is the only place it is found. Cardiac muscle tissue is made up of **interlaced fibres** which help the nervous impulses sent and controlled by the brain to regulate our pulse rate.

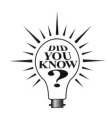

When muscles work in pairs they are said to be **antagonists** *or to work antagonistically. The biceps and triceps are one example of antagonists. The quadriceps and hamstrings are another.*

> *Hints and Tips*
> *There are three types of muscle tissue:*
> - *voluntary (skeletal) – which we can control*
> - *involuntary (smooth) – over which we have no control*
> - *cardiac – which is found only in the heart (as long as it has a good blood supply, cardiac muscle never tires).*

Muscle fibres

As we have seen, muscles are made up of many small muscle cells or muscle fibres. These come in two types known as **fast twitch** and **slow twitch**. We all have both types handed down from our parents in our genes, but the proportion or combination of each is important in terms of sport and physical education.

Fast twitch and slow twitch

Slow twitch fibres are deep red and have a good oxygen supply, which is important for the working muscles. They contract slowly but can work for long periods while under great stress. Fast twitch fibres are white and work much more quickly, though they also tire much quicker.

The longer you can work, the more slow twitch fibres you have. The faster you work, the more fast twitch fibres you have, but you will get tired quicker.

Muscles are attached to bones by **tendons**. They are attached at both ends. One end is called the origin and is fixed to something that is rigid or stable. The other end, which is called the insertion, is fixed to the end that moves. When muscles are relaxed they are long and thin. When they contract they get shorter and thicker.

Muscle tone

The muscle cells need to rest, but they never all rest at the same time. Even when we are asleep some are ready for action. This is known as **muscle tone**. It takes a lot of energy to maintain this action, and the speed with which we use this energy is known as our metabolic rate. Tendons are not made of muscle fibre or we would burn up even more energy in this way.

One of the important jobs that the skeleton does is to provide an attachment for our muscles.

> ### Hints and Tips
> - In order for our joints to move they must be held together with ligaments (which join bone to bone) and tendons (which join muscle to bone).
> - Cartilage covers the ends of bones to prevent rubbing (friction).

It is important to understand the link between bones, joints, ligaments, muscles, tendons and cartilage. You should also learn the movement possibilities about a joint as well as muscular strength and muscular endurance. Additionally, it is important to understand how the balance of both fast and slow twitch fibres can affect a person's potential and ability in sport. Finally, muscle tone is important in terms of rest and readiness and how it can affect a person's posture.

> ### Hints and Tips
> - Hypertrophy is when muscles get bigger.
> - Atrophy is when muscles get smaller.
> Make sure you are able to describe the functions of the muscles and how they may be used in your sport.

Muscles of the upper body

You are required to know about four main muscle groups in this area and it is important to understand exactly what the specification requires – that is 'Recognise and describe, with examples, the functions and relate their use to particular sports.'

The **trapezius** is the muscle that we use to lift, rotate or brace back the shoulder. Any movement that raises the shoulder – for example, raising a tennis racket above the head – uses the trapezius.

The **latissimus dorsi** is a big and very powerful muscle. It is used in any action that involves drawing the arm back and inwards towards the body (adduction). Examples might be the lat pull down, or bent over rowing in weight training, or in competition rowing.

In the front of the body the major muscle group with which we are concerned is the **pectoralis major**. It is easy to describe the location as it covers the chest and is involved with the adduction of the arm, drawing it forwards and rotating it inwards. An example of this movement would be rotating the arm forward in front crawl.

Finally, the **deltoid** can be recognised by the fact that it helps to give the rounded shape to the shoulder. The action of this muscle is that of abduction. It is responsible for raising the shoulder and lifting the arm above the head – for example, a catching action above the head in netball or basketball.

Muscles of the lower body

The **abdominal muscles** are easy to recognise and are used to create movements such as bending forward (flexion) or rotating your trunk from side to side. Movements in games often require sports people to rotate at the waist – for example, in racket games.

The **gluteus maximus** is a powerful muscle that forms the buttocks and is used to pull the leg backwards (extension), an action often used in many sports. An example might be an arabesque in gymnastics.

Hints and Tips
- *Make sure you can identify the muscles for recall questions.*
- *Make sure you are able to describe the functions of the muscles and explain how they may be used in your sport.*
- *The questions which ask you to describe or explain usually carry higher marks.*

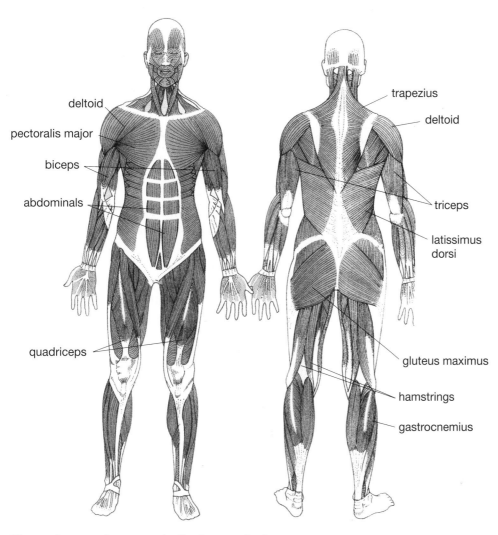

deltoid

pectoralis major

biceps

abdominals

quadriceps

trapezius

deltoid

triceps

latissimus dorsi

gluteus maximus

hamstrings

gastrocnemius

The major muscle groups in the human body

It's easier to remember the muscles if you chunk them into three blocks and remember them. Start at the top and work downwards.

Remembering 11 muscles

Back and bottom = 3
Trapezius
Latissimus Dorsi
Gluteuls

Front upper body and arms = 5
Deltoid
Pectorals
Abdominals
Biceps
Triceps

Legs = 3
Quadriceps
Hamstrings
Gastrocnemius

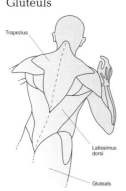

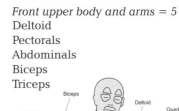

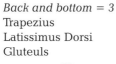

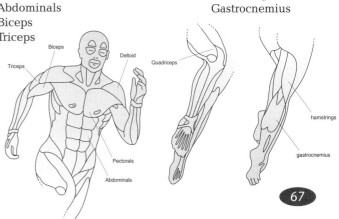

Muscles of the limbs

The muscles of the limbs are important not only because of the actions they perform but also because they are used in the specification as examples of antagonistic pairs, and are therefore always looked at in respect of their actions with each other. In the arms we have the **biceps** and the **triceps**. It is important to remember the fact that muscles can pull but they cannot push. The biceps are located at the front of the upper arm and are used to flex (bend) the arm. The triceps are found at the back of the upper arm and are used to extend (straighten) the arm. When the biceps contract the triceps relax. When the triceps contract the biceps relax. They are known as antagonistic pairs.

There are many examples of this action in sport. One of the most common would be in ball games such as netball and basketball. A player raises his or her arm bent (flexion) ready to shoot the ball, then straightens (extends) the arm, and follows through to direct the shot at the target.

In the lower limbs the same sort of relationship takes place between the **quadriceps** and the **hamstrings**. The quadriceps are the large kicking muscles at the top of the front of the legs. The hamstrings are found at the back of the legs running from the pelvis to the tibia. Like the biceps in the arm, the hamstrings flex (bend) the limb and are therefore very important in running, especially sprinting. The quadriceps and hamstrings are another example of antagonistic pairs. When the hamstrings contract to bend the leg at the knee, the quadriceps relax. When the quadriceps contract to straighten the leg, the hamstrings relax. There are many sporting examples of the use of these muscles – for example, the quadriceps straighten the leg to kick a ball, and the hamstrings bend the leg in any walking or running action.

Finally there is the **gastrocnemius** muscle, more commonly called the calf muscle, which is used to point your toes (planta flexion). This is an action that happens when we run, which is why this muscle may be sore after a long-distance race such as a marathon.

Hints and Tips

Learn the names and locations of these muscles:
- *trapezius, latissimus dorsi, gluteus maximus, deltoid, pectorals, abdominals, biceps and triceps, quadriceps, hamstrings, gastrocnemius.*

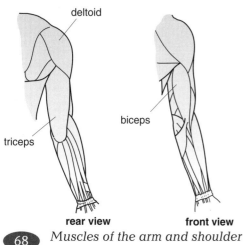

rear view   front view
Muscles of the arm and shoulder

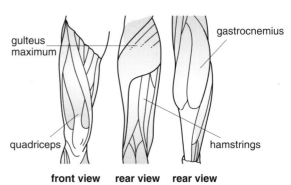

front view   rear view   rear view
Muscles of the leg

Test yourself

Muscles

1. There are **three** different types of muscle fibre, and therefore **three** different types of muscle. Describe briefly each type of muscle, give an example of each, and indicate which type of muscle fibre each muscle is made up of. Arrange your answer in the form of a table. **10 marks**

2. Muscle fibres can influence the types of sports and events we are likely to be good at. Matt C is a 400-metres specialist, an event that requires **anaerobic fitness**. Sports people who specialise in this type of activity are likely to have more _____ _____ muscle fibres, whereas Jill, who plays netball and runs cross-country, which relies more on **aerobic fitness**, will be likely to have more _____ _____ muscle fibres. **2 marks**

3. Ligaments, tendons and cartilage are all involved with joints in the body and therefore have an effect on our ability and potential in sport. Many sports people are affected by injuries to one or more of these. Barrie, for example, had 'cartilage trouble', which prevented him from training and caused him to have an operation. The specialist explained that cartilage is found at the _____ of bones and is there to prevent _____ . **2 marks**

4. Muscles are not attached directly to the skeleton but by a _____ at each end. These help the muscles to pull on bones to flex and extend a joint. In order to do this, one end is fixed rigid and is called the _____ , while the other end is attached to the end that pulls and is called the _____ . **3 marks**

5. Explain briefly what is meant by muscle tone. **1 mark**

6. Look at the diagram on page 67. The deltoid is found over the top and to the side of the shoulder. Describe where the other three of the four muscles in the upper body appear. **3 marks**

7. Describe where the muscles known as the abdominals are found. Then name an exercise that could be used in the Personal Exercise Programme to strengthen this muscle. **2 marks**

8. The biceps and triceps in the arm, and the quadriceps and hamstrings in the legs are examples of antagonistic muscles. Describe what is meant by antagonistic muscles. **1 mark**

9. Choose a sport and describe an action in which the biceps and triceps work in this way. Then choose a sport and describe an action in which the quadriceps and hamstrings work in this way. **6 marks**

Total 30 marks

Section D: Safety

16 Flexibility, risk assessment and posture

For this topic you should study:
- flexibility
- rules and laws
- prevention of injury
- sports injuries and first aid
- posture.

Flexibility

Flexibility is one of the aspects of health-related exercise. It is usually good in the young and poor in the old. It is also often better in females than in males. This can be seen if a comparison is made between the tables for females and males often used to measure flexibility.

So what is flexibility and what do you need to know for the examination? The first thing to learn is how to define the term.

> **Definition**
> **Flexibility** is the range of movement possible at a joint. It is affected by a number of things, including muscle length and the joint structure. **Elasticity** is similar to that in an elastic band, which returns to its normal length after being stretched.

It is also necessary to know how to improve this area of fitness and how to avoid injury.

We stretch our muscles when we warm-up in order to avoid injury when we work. We can improve our flexibility in three ways.

1. By stretching our muscles and holding our stretches for over 30 seconds (static stretching).

2. To bounce into a stretch. This is not recommended because of the risks involved.

3. By using a method called Proprioceptive Neuromuscular Facilitation (PNF), which involves a second person to assist your stretch.

> *Hints and Tips*
> - *Make sure you know about static stretches.*
> - *In order to avoid injury by over-stretching we need to warm-up.*
> - *Injuries to our joints often restrict our flexibility and we need to stretch to get it back again.*
> - *If you are fit you will be able to move your joints through a good range of movement.*

Risks and safety aspects associated with taking part in sport

Injuries can occur in most sports, so it is important to assess the risks and take as many precautions as possible to avoid injury in the first place. The safety aspects in sport are important and many careers have been curtailed because of injury. The specification covers a variety of topics that are broken down under the following headings:

- obeying the rules
- correct clothing
- balanced competition
- warm-up (see page 45).

Obeying the rules

Obeying the rules of the game refers to the fact that if you take part in sport it is your responsibility to show what is often called 'good sporting behaviour'. This implies that you play within the rules of safety and take care not to injure an opponent intentionally. At the highest levels, this has sometimes been brought into question in recent years. For example, football players are sometimes quoted as saying, 'I wouldn't hurt a fellow professional intentionally!'

In serious cases, both at professional and amateur level, players have been taken to court because of 'foul play' that has resulted in serious injury to an opponent. A high tackle in rugby or a tackle over the top of the ball in football might fall into this category.

Hints and Tips

Players are expected to obey the rules, not only so that they are not cautioned or sent off by the officials, but also because playing within the rules helps to prevent injuries.

Correct clothing

The first and most obvious method of injury prevention in most activities is to wear protective clothing of some description. Wearing some of this clothing might be voluntary – for example, skullcaps are worn by *some* rugby players but not by *all* of them. In other situations protective clothing or equipment may be compulsory; shin pads in football are an example of this.

In terms of **risk assessment**, it is important to 'know the obvious'. For example, wearing a wristwatch or jewellery is dangerous both to the person wearing it, a partner or team mate and to an opponent. There are some other obvious, but all too often neglected, items that come into this category. One of these is footwear. Running shoes can be expensive, but modern technology has made it possible to produce training and running shoes that protect the feet and joints much more. A tracksuit is often not considered to be an item of protection, but in cold weather it is essential in helping to prevent pulling cold muscles before activity and preventing getting cold after activity.

Balanced competition

Competition organisers are also obligated to take into account the risks and safety requirements necessary when organising tournaments. This may be as simple as balancing the competition – for example, taking into account the ability or grade of the competitors in combat sports. In a league competition this is taken into account almost automatically with promotion of the strongest teams and relegation of the weaker ones.

In some sports competitors are matched by **weight**. Boxing is the obvious example but other combat sports also use weight categories.

Two of the main methods of categorising for safety are by **gender** and **age**, and there are many examples of both. Most of the sports that involve physical contact (including football and rugby) are played as single gender groupings, as are most of the racket games (table tennis being the exception). However, both tennis and badminton offer mixed competition, as is the case with hockey. In the United States of America, professional boxing has been heavily criticised for allowing some fights between men and women to take place, but it is still an exception rather than the rule.

In school sport, age is one of the main factors in categorising competition as well as gender. However, because of the growth spurt that comes early for some students, age often results in quite unequal competition.

Hints and Tips
- *Make sure you know about risk assessment for all your exercises and sports.*
- *Make sure you know about protective clothing (compulsory/voluntary) for at least one of your sports.*

Sport injuries

However hard we try to avoid injury and whatever risk assessments we take, injury at some time is almost inevitable. It is then important to recognise what are known as the **signs** and **symptoms** of any injury, and to have some knowledge of how to minimise their effects. You will be expected to know about this for your examination.

A sign is something you can see, feel, hear or smell.

A symptom is what the casualty feels and conveys to you.

Earlier in this course we gained a lot of knowledge regarding bones, joints, muscles, ligaments, tendons and cartilage. All this is regarded as underpinning knowledge to help you to understand training and preparation for your sport. It should also help you to understand how to prevent injuries, recognise them if they happen and to know what to do if they *do* happen.

Injuries to the joints

The joint injuries you need to know about include a twisted ankle, dislocations, torn cartilage of the knee and tennis/golf elbow.

A **twisted ankle joint** can come about in most sports, either when competing directly against an opponent in a tackle, or by stepping awkwardly on the ball or the ground. In this injury the fibres of the ligaments and/or tendons are torn loose from their attachment. The **signs** can include swelling and bruising, and the player will be reluctant to put his/her foot on the floor. The **symptoms** include the pain the player will feel at the site of the injury.

A **dislocation** can occur from a blow – that is, from a collision with an opponent or from a fall that causes one of the bones to come out of the joint. The main **sign** will be deformity at the joint, swelling and the inability of the casualty to move the limb. The **symptoms** will be the severe pain felt by the casualty.

A **torn cartilage** can happen when the femur changes direction quickly and traps cartilage that can be torn under the pressure. The **sign** may be that the player cannot straighten the joint. The **symptom** will be great pain felt by the casualty.

Tennis elbow and **golf elbow** are both tendon injuries. Tennis elbow gives pain on the outside of the joint; golf elbow gives pain on the inside.

Hints and Tips
Make sure you can recognise the signs and symptoms of the types of injury explained above.

Soft tissue injuries

A soft tissue injury, more often called a pulled or strained muscle, is a term often used in sport to describe an injury to a muscle that is usually caused by the small fibres being torn away from a tendon (which we know attaches a muscle to a bone). It can happen in a game but is sometimes caused by not warming-up properly.

Fractures

A **fracture** is a broken or cracked bone. The signs will include the noise of the break. The symptoms include pain, tenderness, bruising, swelling and deformity.

There are two main types of fracture:

- open (when the bone protrudes through the skin)
- closed (when the bone does not protrude).

Footballer David Beckham broke his metatasal bone when playing a game for Manchester United just weeks before he was due to captain the England squad in the 2002 World Cup. Fortunately, he recovered from his injury in time to take part in Japan.

Skin damage

A **cut** is an open wound. Its importance is dependent on how bad it is and/or where it is. In some sports, rugby for example, players must leave the field in the event of being cut and cannot return until the cut has been repaired. Infection can be serious both to the player and to the person dealing with the injury, so special gloves are worn by trainers and physiotherapists dealing with these injuries. The signs are usually obvious, but the player may have pain as a symptom. A **graze** is when the top layers of skin are rubbed away often caused by sliding actions, especially on artificial surfaces such as astro-turf. Dirt and infection may cause further problems.

Blisters are caused by friction and are formed to protect the area while new skin is growing beneath.

Bruises are caused by bleeding internally and are usually caused by blows or twisting at the joints.

Hints and Tips
Remember the **RICE** *principle:*
Rest – *stop playing or training*
Ice – *place an ice pack on the injury*
Compression – *use pressure on the ice pack*
Elevate – *raise the injured region (and rest for 24 hours).*

Hypothermia

Hypothermia occurs when the body temperature falls below about 35°C. When it drops to below 26°C, this usually results in death. Some sports take place in extreme conditions, snow or water for example, and this can result in exposure to severe cold that in turn can bring about this condition. Shivering and cold, pale skin are symptoms. Extra layers of clothing help to keep out the cold.

Dehydration

Dehydration can occur in most sports but is common in those of long duration and/or that take place in extreme heat. Sports people are now much more aware of this condition, and most players and competitors take on plenty of fluids, often water or isotonic drinks. It is also possible to become dehydrated when training excessively and/or by wearing extra clothing to lose weight by sweating. Dehydration can be recognised by tiredness, nausea and dizziness.

Unconsciousness

Loss of consciousness is a result of interference with the brain and can be caused by a reduced supply of blood, heart attack, stroke, shock, hypothermia, epilepsy, suffocation or drowning.

There are many reasons why a person can become unconscious in sport, but it is most often brought about by a blow to the head or to the jaw. In boxing this is the aim of the activity, but in games such as football it can come about by a collision often when heading the ball.

Concussion

As with unconsciousness, concussion usually happens because of a blow to the head or to the jaw. The signs might be that the player will become unconscious, cold and have a high pulse rate. He/she may be unaware of what is happening and should not be allowed to continue the activity.

DID YOU KNOW?

- *Channel swimmers grease up to keep out the cold.*
- *Women feel the cold less than men because they have an extra layer of fat.*

Hints and Tips

DR ABC will help you to remember the stages to follow if someone is unconscious:
D *is for danger – either to the injured person or to the rescuer*
R *is for response – check the injured person for a response*
A *is for airway – check the airway is clear*
B *is for breathing – check for breathing*
  - *can you see or feel the chest rise?*
  - *can you hear breathing?*
C *is for circulation – check the pulse.*

Posture

Definition
Posture is the ability to maintain the relative position of parts of the body. The function that allows us to achieve this is muscle tone.

Bad posture
Some people have specific medical causes for what might be called bad posture, but for many it is often to do with simply not holding our bodies correctly, carrying extra weight or having muscles that are not strong enough or become tired quickly. Bad posture is also caused by other activities such as driving or sitting bent over a desk. Footwear has been mentioned earlier as being important with regard to safety, but it is often blamed for causing bad posture, especially high heels.

Good posture
As with many physical activities, it is easy to see what is good posture because it looks good. Whether sitting, walking, running or standing, good posture appears elegant, balanced, comfortable and effortless. The head and shoulders should be well balanced, the spine straight above the hips and the feet square to the ground. These points are emphasised in yoga.

Maintaining good posture
Many aspects of training have been covered and all of these contribute to good posture. The main activities for maintaining good posture include light weight training to improve and maintain muscle tone, the discipline of working and lifting correctly, and a most important but often neglected aspect of health-related exercise, flexibility.

Some people take part in sport because it:
- *makes them look good*
- *makes them feel good*
- *enhances their body shape.*

This is all to do with posture.

Yoga helps to prevent poor posture and to develop good posture.

Hints and Tips
Be able to describe and explain the importance of good posture.

Test yourself

Flexibility, risk assessment and posture

1. Flexibility is an area of health-related exercise. Complete the following definition and fill in the gaps. Flexibility is the _____ of _____ possible at a joint.

    2 marks

2. In our profiles we have a number of people who take part in sport for various reasons: Albert, our 92 year-old marathon runner; Teresa, the 50 year-old grandmother and Derek, our 50 year-old ex-British champion. Rank these three in order starting with the most flexible. Explain your reasons.

    5 marks

3. Garry, the YTS footballer, is very competitive and wants to be successful. His motto is 'play hard but play fair'. Why is it important for players to play fair and within the rules in sport?

    1 mark

4. Wearing protective clothing can help to prevent injury. Name a sport, or sports. Now give two pieces of equipment that are not compulsory but are used to prevent injury in that sport. Then name one compulsory piece of equipment used to prevent injury.

    3 marks

5. Apart from wearing special equipment, there are other safety measures in sport. Name a sport and list three things in that sport you should not do because of the safety risk. Write them as statements – for example, in trampolining you should not chew gum while bouncing.

    3 marks

6. Give the names of three sports that are played at secondary school level including one that is played only as single gender (for example, football is played as only boys' football or girls' football), one that is played as mixed gender (for example, tennis is played with just boys, just girls, or mixed), and one in which boys and girls may compete in open competition.

    3 marks

7. Ian, our 30 year-old ex-footballer, has become a sports physiotherapist. It is very important for him to know about signs and symptoms. What is the difference between a sign and a symptom?

    2 marks

8. During a football match Paul, one of the players, falls heavily on his shoulder. Ian runs across to him and asks him about the incident, but he can already see that the shoulder is deformed and that Paul is in a lot of pain. He cannot move the arm and it is very tender. What two types of injury could Paul have sustained?

    2 marks

9. Paul says he thought he heard a noise as he hit the ground. What might this confirm for Ian?

    1 mark

    Total 22 marks

Test yourself further

Flexibility, risk assessment and posture

1. Derek, our ex-national champion, has joined a golf club and has played regularly over recent weeks. He has a pain in his elbow. Exactly where might this be if, as he suspects, it is golf elbow? **1 mark**

2. Derek slipped off a curb while out jogging. He thought he had sprained his ankle. Give two likely symptoms that might confirm this. **2 marks**

3. Derek has been somewhat injury prone during his sporting years. He once had a fracture where the bone actually pierced the skin. What type of fracture is this? **1 mark**

4. Another type of injury that can happen at a joint occurs when one or more bones become displaced. What is the name given to this type of injury? **1 mark**

5. Cuts are often a cause for concern not only for those who get cut, but also for those who treat them. What precaution might a person who is treating a cut take to prevent catching an infection from the wound? **1 mark**

6. Derek takes part in many outdoor activities such as skiing, canoeing and camping. In cold weather he stresses the importance of wearing the correct clothing because of the risks. What risks does he mean? **1 mark**

7. If a person is suffering from the condition in question 6, name two symptoms that might indicate this. **2 marks**

8. Training and competing in hot weather also have their problems, especially regarding dehydration. What precautions can a competitor take to try to prevent this? **1 mark**

9. Give two examples of the symptoms of dehydration. **2 marks**

10. Unconsciousness can happen in sport for a variety of reasons, but what exactly is unconsciousness? **1 mark**

11. DRABC are the letters used to remember what to do when a person is unconscious. What does each letter stand for? **5 marks**

12. Concussion can result from a blow to the head or a collision. Give two examples of a symptom of concussion. **2 marks**

13. Posture can be affected by a number of things. Give three possible reasons for bad posture. **3 marks**

14. Describe briefly in your own words what is meant by good posture. **1 mark**

15. Give an example of a training activity that will help to improve posture. **1 mark**

Total 25 marks

17 Motor skills and drugs in sport

For this topic you should study:
- the six motor skills
- drugs
- the effects of smoking and alcohol on health and performance
- socially unacceptable drugs
- performance enhancing drugs.

Total fitness

For a person to have total fitness, aspects other than physical fitness are involved. We have considered psychological fitness in terms of stress, and social fitness in terms of co-operation (see pages 1 to 6). Emotional fitness and spiritual fitness are also required. Total physical fitness includes the five health-related factors plus the six skill-related or motor skill factors described below.

Ability in these six factors can influence our chance of success in certain activities and they are very important for success in sport. They are sometimes referred to as sports fitness, but technically they are known as the six motor skills.

The six motor skills

Agility

> **Definition**
> **Agility** is the ability to change the position of the body quickly and to control the movement of the whole body.

Some sports need some skills more than others. In terms of moving the whole body quickly, rugby would be a good example when running for the try line and side stepping (dodging) an opponent. In a similar way, netball would require agility when dodging to get free from an opponent to make yourself available for a pass.

An example of static balance is holding a headstand position, while an example of dynamic balance is completing gymnastics movements along a gymnastics bench.

Balance

> **Definition**
> **Balance** is defined as the ability to retain the centre of mass (gravity) of the body above the base of support, with reference to static (stationary) or dynamic (changing) conditions of movement, shape and orientation. In simple terms it could be described as maintaining equilibrium while at rest or moving.

Hints and Tips
- *It is important to learn the definitions of each of the six motor skills.*
- *Make sure you know which sports each can be applied to.*
- *Be able to relate each skill to your sport.*

Co-ordination

> **Definition**
> **Co-ordination** is the ability to use two or more body parts together.

The most common combination of co-ordination in sport is hand–eye. For example, a player catches a ball in his or her hand, or hits it with a bat or other implement. The second most common type is foot–eye. For example, a player strikes a ball or controls it with his or her foot. Head–eye co-ordination happens frequently in football and volleyball. The chest and knee are also used in this way.

Power

> **Definition**
> **Power** is the ability to do strength performances quickly:
> power = strength × speed.

All sports activities that require strength, and all sports activities that require speed, are almost certainly going to require 'power'. A shot putter who is strong and slow will not win at the highest levels. Sprinters have speed, but they also need strength and the top sprinters can be seen to be powerful.

Reaction time

> **Definition**
> **Reaction time** is the time between the presentation of a stimulus and the onset of a movement.

An obvious example of reaction time is the time between the sound of the starter's pistol (the stimulus) and the reaction of the sprinters on their blocks. Less obvious examples are when the stimulus is seen rather than heard. In combat sports, players attempt to make a move, but opponents react to counter it. Tennis players strike the ball and opponents react to attempt a return. Players often use deception to shorten the amount of time the opponent has to react.

Speed

> **Definition**
> **Speed** is the differential rate at which an individual is able to perform a movement or cover a distance in a period of time.

The best example is the 100-metres sprint, where the sprinter has to cover the distance in a short period of time. In golf, players try to get the head of the club to move at great speed when it makes contact with the ball and in racket sports when contact is made with the racket. The arm speed to bowl or throw (generate power) in baseball and cricket are examples in these sports.

> *Hints and Tips*
> *Make sure you are able to give examples of how to improve speed in your sport.*

Drugs in sport

What are drugs?

> **Definition**
> A **drug** is a substance that can be taken in a variety of ways to produce expected and welcome physical and/or psychological effects on the person taking it. It may cause some effects that are both unpleasant and unwanted. These are known as side effects.

There are a number of categories of drugs and many are used in everyday life. Some of these can affect our health, both in terms of improving it in the form of a medicine, and socially in terms of nicotine and alcohol for example. Some drugs have side effects on our health and our ability to exercise.

Side effects of taking drugs

Cancer is closely associated as a side effect of smoking, but coronary heart disease (CHD) is a much more common and life-threatening side effect of smoking. Smoking damages the heart, reduces the ability of the blood to carry oxygen and damages the blood vessels. It therefore damages the cardiovascular system, the most important aspect of health-related exercise. It also increases blood pressure and damages the alveoli in the lungs, and therefore damages the respiratory system. These are all vitally important to sports people and people who are health conscious.

The use of alcohol can cause dehydration and one of the long-term effects is cirrhosis of the liver. This can result in death.

Many sports people – especially footballers – have recently admitted alcohol abuse. George Best, the ex-Manchester United footballer, thought by many to be the greatest footballer of all time, admits to being an alcoholic. His addiction (an illness) to alcohol so seriously affected his liver function, a side effect of this drug, that he had a liver transplant after having special pellets sown into his stomach to make him ill if he drank alcohol. So alcohol is also a factor that affects performance.

> *Hints and Tips*
> - *Nicotine and alcohol are addictive. Addiction is classed as a side effect.*
> - *Alcohol is a banned drug in some sports (for example, shooting), as it can be used to give a calming effect. It is also banned in motor racing because it slows down reaction time.*

Why do sports people take drugs?

Sports people may decide to take drugs because they can enhance their performance. Although the decision to take drugs may be made by the athlete, he or she may be encouraged by his or her coach, other athletes or managers. Taking certain drugs may help athletes to win, make a lot of money or perform at a level they could not reach without the aid of drugs. A number of sports have been tainted because athletes have taken drugs and subsequently been banned after tests have proved positive.

Performance enhancing drugs fall into two categories:

- prohibited substances
- prohibited methods.

Prohibited substances

Stimulants

Stimulants include a number of substances that can be found in some medicines that are available over the counter in any chemist's shop. In sport these may be taken to stimulate the central nervous system (CNS) and they can also be used to offset the effects of lactic acid.

Side effects that may be produced by stimulants include insomnia, irregular heartbeat, increased heart rate and high blood pressure.

Narcotics and analgesics

As we have seen, there are many risks of injury that sports people face. In order to get back from injury quickly, some athletes may resort to taking a short cut by taking drugs. **Narcotics** or **analgesics**, of which there are many, can help them to do this by giving relief from pain, and enabling them to continue to train and compete. This, however, may increase the risk of making the injury worse. It is because of this that these types of drug are on the banned list. Narcotics and analgesics also have side effects including loss of concentration, balance and co-ordination (motor skills), which sports people can ill afford if they are to compete at the highest levels.

Narcotics and analgesics include heroin, methadone, pethidine and morphine.

Anabolic steroids

Probably the best known of the performance enhancing drugs is the group known as **anabolic steroids**. These drugs help to increase muscle mass and bone growth, and, as they also allow the athlete to train harder, the result will be a quick and large increase in muscular strength and power. Many of the specific names of steroids are well known because they are often in the sports news – for example, testosterone, nandrolone, stanozonol and bodlenone.

Steroids have their side effects, too. Some of the more well known of these are deepening of the voice and growing facial hair, most noticeable in women. There are others including more risk of muscle injuries, heart attacks, strokes and high blood pressure, mood swings, aggression, the face can become puffy, liver disease can develop, and women can become infertile. Steroids can also cause death.

Diuretics
There are sports that require the competitors to fit into weight categories – for example, boxing. In order to lose weight, **diuretics** are used, which can help sports people to lose weight quickly by increasing the amount of urine produced. A common side effect is dehydration, but diuretics can also cause dizziness, muscle cramps, headaches and nausea, and, in the long-term, kidney damage. These drugs can also be taken to mask other banned drugs.

Peptide, chemical and physical manipulation
Peptide, chemical and physical manipulation have a similar effect to steroids, and also speed up recovery from injury. They are also used because they increase the number of red blood cells, which means the athlete can get more oxygen to the muscles. One of the comparatively new drugs is human growth hormone (hGH). This can produce the same effects as steroids, but has the advantage of fewer side effects and is more difficult to detect. Erythropoietin (EPO) increases the production of red blood cells, therefore creating more haemoglobin. A side effect of EPO is that it thickens the blood and can therefore cause a heart attack or a stroke. This is another drug that is difficult to detect.

The **International Olympic Committee (IOC)** has strict rules for dealing with prohibited substances and insists on random urine tests being taken both during and out of the competitive season. The sample is split into two and tests are performed on the first one. If any trace of a banned drug is found, the second sample is tested in the presence of the athlete. Other ruling bodies have their own procedures, so there is no common way of testing. In February 1999, the IOC proposal to have a single international anti-doping agency with a blanket two-year ban if found guilty was turned down by the governing bodies of cycling, tennis and football.

Prohibited methods
As well as banned drugs, there are **prohibited methods** and these too are difficult to detect. Blood doping has been around for a number of years and involves an athlete training at high altitude to encourage the production of red blood cells. Up to two pints of blood are then taken from the athlete and the red blood cells are frozen. The blood is re-introduced into the bloodstream near to the day of a big competition and this can raise the athlete's performance by up to 20%.

Hints and Tips
Make sure you learn the various categories of drugs:
- *stimulants*
- *narcotics and analgesics*
- *anabolic steroids*
- *diuretics*
- *peptide, chemical and physical manipulation.*

Test yourself

Motor skills and drugs in sport

1. Derek and Matt S are both former national champions in their own particular sports, Derek in a water sport and Matt in a combat sport. In a discussion they are debating the order of importance of each of the motor skills in their particular sport. Derek thinks co-ordination was the most important for him; Matt thinks speed was the most important for him. Choose a sport from two of the six National Curriculum areas: games, swimming, dance, gymnastics, athletics and outdoor and adventurous activities. List the six motor skills in order of importance for each sport, starting with the most important. **12 marks**

2. Take the two skills that come out top for you and write a definition for each of them. **2 marks**

3. Luke is a national junior champion in a sport in which athletes are reputed to take drugs. From the definition of a drug, what might these athletes expect to get from taking them? **1 mark**

4. Luke, Matt C and Garry all want to reach the top in their sports so they do not smoke. Coronary heart disease (CHD) is the most common side effect of smoking. What is the next most common? **1 mark**

5. Give three side effects that smoking has on the cardiovascular system. **3 marks**

6. Give one side effect that smoking has on the respiratory system. **1 mark**

7. Excessive use of alcohol can damage the liver. Which of the following is the liver condition caused by too much alcohol?
A Lordosis   B Kyfosis   C Cirrhosis   D Scoliosis **1 mark**

8. Apart from the answer included in the definition of a drug, why might athletes at the highest level of sport take drugs? **1 mark**

9. Drugs that are banned fall into two categories. What are these catagories? **2 marks**

10. A stimulant is a type of drug. Why might an athlete take a stimulant? **1 mark**

11. Give one side effect of taking a stimulant. **1 mark**

12. Injury is often a problem for athletes and there are some drugs that can help them to recover more quickly. Give an example of such a drug. **1 mark**

13. Testosterone, nandrolone, stanozonol and bodlenone are all a type of what? **1 mark**

14. New drugs are being developed all the time, and one of the new ones that can produce startling effects has the initials hGH. What does hGH stand for? **1 mark**

15. The IOC is a ruling body that carries out drug testing. What does IOC stand for? **1 mark**

Total 30 marks

Section E: Examination preparation

18 Final examination preparation and tips

For this topic you should study:
- all the topics
- all the 'Hints and Tips'
- any topic that needs special attention (by checking your answers to the questions).

Knowledge recall

Some of the questions on the written paper will be what is known as **knowledge recall**. The first of these questions will be multiple choice. These will require you to recall some knowledge you have learned and enter the correct letter in a box. Other questions will require you to slot in the correct answer, perhaps by writing it on a line, by filling in a blank space or box, or by choosing the correct answer from several options that are given. To revise for these you will need to learn the facts – for example, the parts of the heart and the respiratory system. The muscles and the bones are two other areas where you will need to use your knowledge recall for the names of the parts and the places where they are found.

How to remember
Some students find it easy to remember things, and for them the knowledge recall questions are quite easy. If you find it difficult there are two methods that can be used to help you:

1. Grouping
You can learn some of the things you have been taught as groups of words. Health-related exercise, for example, will have been introduced as five areas, so if you have a question that perhaps gives you two and you are asked to name the others, you know how many you are looking for.

2. Ordering
You could also learn the five areas of health-related exercise and think of these always in the same order. For example:

- cardiovascular fitness (the most important aspect)
- muscular strength
- muscular endurance
- flexibility
- body composition.

Additionally, you could use a mnemonic – that is, make up something to remind you of the words you need. Below is an example of a mnemonic you might use in order to learn the six components of skill fitness.

A	**A**gility
B	**B**alance
C	**C**o-ordination
Peter	**P**ower
Robert	**R**eaction time
Sarah	**S**peed

If you make up your own mnemonics you will find it even easier.

Now make up a mnemonic to remember the regions of the spine.

How to explain

Questions that use the word **explain** are the questions used to differentiate – in other words, they give an opportunity for the A and A* candidates to demonstrate that they really **understand** and can **apply** their knowledge. Throughout this book, every opportunity is taken to try to relate the information to real situations. This is what you will be required to do to get good answers and full marks for the more difficult questions. In these higher-mark questions you will have to be able to explain your answers by taking the knowledge you have and applying it in a scenario-type question. This takes a lot of practice, which is why so many of the questions in this book are based on scenarios. You could practise this by working on your own scenarios when you play or train for your own sport. When you swim a length of the swimming pool, run around an athletics track or train for your team game, how many aspects of your Edexcel course can you relate to what you have done?

Number of marks for each question

The number of marks for each question will be indicated on the examination paper (as they are indicated in the questions in this book). Therefore you can usually work out how many points or words to include to get full marks for the question.

A final point

Remember that each part of the specification will be examined, so revise it all. Do not miss bits out – and good luck!

> **Hints and Tips**
> - *If you cannot remember a definition, write it out in your own words.*
> - *Learn the parts of the heart. This is often a subject that carries many marks.*
> - *Learn to explain your answers. Do not just recall information.*
> - *If examples are required, the 'Did you know' points in this book will help, but also use examples from your own training and competitions.*

Section F: Answers to questions

Reasons for taking part in physical activity (page 7)

1. Psychological, physical and social.   **3 marks**
2.

psychological	physical	social
Elaine	Jack	Derek
relieves stress/tension	improves body shape	stimulating

     3 marks
3. Luke, Matt C, Garry, Duncan (any three of these four characters).   **3 marks**
4. Derek, Teresa, Elaine, Jack, Ian, Norbert, Albert, Jill, Audrey, Anita, Louise, Ann, Barrie, Lionel (any four of these).   **4 marks**
5. Work, play, social life, holidays (any two).   **2 marks**
6. Not being able to do their job properly.   **1 mark**
7. Achieving training target zone.   **1 mark**
8. See definitions on pages 5 and 6.   **4 marks**
9. Change into sports clothes, shower, powder/deodorant (any two).   **2 marks**
10. Athlete's foot = fungal. Verrucae = viral.   **2 marks**
11. Plantar wart.   **1 mark**
12. Recognised by flaky skin between the toes. Treated using powder or cream. Passed on by sharing towels, socks, training shoes.   **3 marks**
13. Swimming pools.   **1 mark**

     Total 30 marks

Body composition (page 12)

1. Cardiovascular fitness, muscular strength, muscular endurance, flexibility.   **4 marks**
2. The percentage of body weight that is fat, muscle and bone.   **1 mark**
3. Height, sex, bone structure, muscle girth (any three).   **3 marks**
4. Audrey might have a heavier bone structure and be more muscular due to competing at high levels of performance in her sport (swimming).   **2 marks**
5. He has no excess fat.   **1 mark**
6. Too much body composition as fat.   **1 mark**
7. Obese.   **1 mark**
8. Luke: advantage/strength to throw further.
   Garry: disadvantage/less mobility, less agility playing in mid-field.
   Matt C: disadvantage/too much extra weight would slow him down over 800m.   **3 marks**
9. Decrease kilocalorie intake, increase kilocalorie energy expenditure, combination of both.   **3 marks**
10. High energy use.   **1 mark**
11. Less speed, endurance and agility.   **3 marks**
12. Ladies' marathon (or similar answer).   **1 mark**
13. Jockey/boxer (or similar answer).   **1 mark**

     Total 25 marks

Diet (page 16)

1. 1 sugars, 2 starch.   **2 marks**
2. Simple = sugars; complex = starch.   **2 marks**
3. Simple.   **1 mark**
4. Complex.   **1 mark**
5. Potatoes, bread, rice.   **1 mark**
6. Complex.   **1 mark**
7. Protein, to build muscle, found in meat, fish, dairy products, milk, eggs.   **3 marks**
8. Fat.   **1 mark**
9. Carbohydrates (47%); fat (30%); protein (15%).   **3 marks**
10. Tablets.   **1 mark**

11. Calcium (teeth/bones); iron (red blood cells).   **2 marks**
12. Carbohydrate.   **1 mark**
13. In the last training week, cut down on carbohydrate early in the week, then stock up later in the week.   **2 marks**
14. Fat.   **1 mark**
15. To prevent dehydration.   **1 mark**
16. Fibre; prevents constipation.   **2 marks**

    Total 25 marks

Somatotypes (page 20)

1. Somatotype.   **1 mark**
2. Height, weight, bone size, muscle girth, body fat (any three).   **3 marks**
3. Endomorph, mesomorph, ectomorph.   **3 marks**
4. Ectomorph (or ectomorphic) mesomorph.   **1 mark**
5. Mesomorphic endomorph.   **2 marks**
6. Fat, muscle.   **2 marks**
7.

Sport	Somatotype
Tennis at Wimbledon	mesomorphic ectomorph
100m sprint (Olympic final)	mesomorph
Flat race jockey	ectomorph
Golf (the Open)	variety, often endomorphic mesomorph
Football (midfielder)	mesomorph
Basketball (rebounder)	mesomorphic ectomorph
World's strongest man	mesomorphic endomorph
Sumo wrestler	endomorph

    8 marks
8. Luke and Garry – mesomorph; Matt C – ectomorph.   **3 marks**
9. Ectomorph.   **1 mark**
10. Weight training.   **1 mark**

    Total 25 marks

Cardiovascular fitness 1 (page 24)

1, 2, 3. See diagram below.   **9 marks**
(5 for question 1, 2 each for questions 2 and 3)

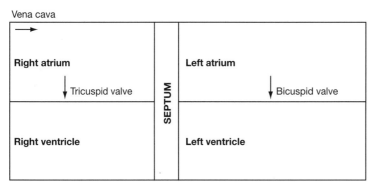

4. vena cava
right atrium
tricuspid valve
right ventricle
semilunar valve
pulmonary artery
lungs
pulmonary vein
left atrium
bicuspid valve
left ventricle
semilunar valve
aorta   **12 marks**

5. The septum divides the heart in two and keeps blood separate.
   The problem is that oxygenated and de-oxygenated blood would mix. **2 marks**
6. Arteries normally carry oxygenated blood away from the heart.
   The pulmonary artery is unique because it carries de-oxygenated blood
   away from the heart. Veins normally carry de-oxygenated blood to the
   heart. The pulmonary vein is unique because it carries oxygenated blood to
   the heart. **2 marks**
   Total 25 marks

Cardiovascular fitness 2 (page 27)
1. Heart/blood/blood vessels. **3 marks**
2. Deoxygenated/muscles/capillaries/oxygenated/de-oxgenated/venules/vein/
   right atrium/vena cava. **9 marks**
3. Lungs/pulmonary/de-oxygenated/pulmonary vein/vein/oxygenated. **6 marks**
4. Left atrium/bicuspid/left ventricle/aorta/semilunar. **5 marks**
5. Blood cells/pulsate/high/oxygen/haemoglobin/red blood cells/oxygen/
   platelets/bacteria. **9 marks**
   Total 32 marks

How training and fitness affect the heart (page 31)
1. False. It is the number of times the heart beats per minute. **1 mark**
2. True. **1 mark**
3. Exercise/blood pressure/overfat/smoking/eating/anger/age/gender
   (women are likely to have higher pulse rates) (any three). **3 marks**
4. Lower. **1 mark**
5. Anita = 220 – 66 = 154; Louise = 220 – 44 = 176. **3 marks**
6. The amount of blood pumped with each beat of the heart. **1 mark**
7. It increases. **1 mark**
8. CO = HR × SV **1 mark**
9. CO and SV increase, HR decreases. **3 marks**
10. She will be able to carry more oxygen because she has more red blood cells
    and haemoglobin. She will be able to get rid of more carbon dioxide quicker. **2 marks**
11. It will enable her to play and not get tired easily. **1 mark**
12. To establish her fitness level; to set a safe programme; to monitor fitness over
    a period of time (or two similar answers). **2 marks**
13. Resting pulse rate = pulse at rest;
    working pulse rate = pulse while working/as soon as she stops;
    recovery rate = time taken to reach resting pulse rate after stopping exercise.
    Resting pulse rate and recovery rate monitor fitness level.
    Working pulse rate measures the level of intensity of work. **5 marks**
    Total 25 marks

Respiratory fitness (page 35)
1. Breathe in/intercostal muscles/contract/upwards and outwards/diaphragm/
   flattens/lowers/dome shape/upwards and outwards/pressure inside/air
   rushes in. **10 marks**
2. A = pleural membrane, B = trachea, C = bronchus, D = bronchiole,
   E = alveoli. **5 marks**
3. Hairs in nose; warmed by blood vessels; moistened by water vapour; to allow
   alveoli to work efficiently. **4 marks**
4. Oxygen in 20%, out 16%. Carbon dioxide in 0.4%, out 4%. **2 marks**
5. Glucose + Oxygen → Energy + Carbon dioxide + Water **2 marks**
6. Tidal volume = amount they breathe with each breath.
   Vital capacity = The largest amount of air that can be breathed in and out
   of the lungs by the most forceful inspiration and expiration (or simple words). **2 marks**
   Total 25 marks

The effects of exercise (page 41)
1. Rise in pulse rate/more blood required.
   Breathing quicker/deeper/more oxygen required.
   Temperature rise/exercise = energy = heat. **6 marks**
2. Lactic acid/oxygen. **2 marks**
3. Oxygen debt. **1 mark**
4. Aerobic/anaerobic. **2 marks**
5. Aerobic = production of energy with oxygen.
   Anaerobic = production of energy without oxygen. **2 marks**
6. Anaerobic. **1 mark**
7. Aerobic: lower intensity, do not get out of breath.
   Anaerobic: higher intensity, get breathless. **2 marks**
8. Anaerobic – netball; aerobic – cross-country. **2 marks**
9. Improved stroke volume – heart pumps more blood per beat.
   More capillaries around her heart – more efficient gas exchange.
   More efficient CV system – heart recovers quicker/lower resting heart rate. **6 marks**
10. CHD risk is reduced; Jill can work harder for longer (any one). **1 mark**
Total 25 marks

The principles of training (page 46)
1. The programme must be planned. This will ensure it takes place. **2 marks**
2. What Barrie wants from the programme (health/fitness); how he is going to achieve it; when/where he trains; facilities; cost; training alone; how he will reach his targets (any three). **3 marks**
3. Specificity. **1 mark**
4. Frequency. Training six days a week, which is more than enough.
   Intensity. Trains at about the same intensity each day – not good enough to improve on what he now has.
   Time. Spends enough time (over twenty minutes) to keep fit.
   Type. Uses aerobic training and cross-training. **4 marks**
5. Thresholds of training – 60% lower threshold; 80% upper threshold.
   Target zone – working at a high enough intensity, 60% to 80% is the target range. **3 marks**
6. Max HR = 220 – age
   Max HR = 220 – 50 = 170
   $170 \times 60\% = 102$; $170 \times 80\% = 136$ **3 marks**
7. Progression. **1 mark**
8. Working PR; resting PR; recovery rate. **3 marks**
9. Increase the intensity of the sessions or overload. **1 mark**
10. Warm-up; main activity; cool down. **3 marks**
11. Reversibility. **1 mark**
Total 25 marks

Methods of training (page 50)
1. Swimming/cycling/brisk walking/target zone/77/102/aerobic or CV fitness. **7 marks**
2. Anaerobic/interval/work/intensity/rest. **5 marks**
3. Fartlek/speedplay/intensity. **3 marks**
4. Circuit/endurance/cheap/different/individual. **5 marks**
5. Team game: rugby/tennis.
   Racket game: tennis.
   Other activity: hockey. **3 marks**
Total 23 marks

Muscular strength and muscular endurance (page 53)
1. Muscular strength/ability/muscles/force. **2 marks**
2. Heavy/few. **2 marks**
3. Muscular endurance/ability/voluntary or skeletal/tired. **2 marks**

4. Light/many. **2 marks**
5. Voluntary/skeletal or vice versa. **2 marks**
6. Ability to work; reduce risk of injury; back pain; posture; improve all sport; save life; recover from injury (any three). **3 marks**
7. Contract/isometric/handstand; rugby scrum; tug-of-war (any two)/isotonic. **5 marks**
8. Pull/push. **2 marks**

Total 20 marks

Bones (page 58)
1. Structure/optimum/somatotype. **3 marks**
2. Blood cells/bone marrow. **2 marks**
3. Protect/vital/give the body shape; stand upright; mobility; stability; muscle attachment (any four). **6 marks**
4. Line dancing/weight bearing/osteoporosis. **3 marks**
5. Diet/calcium/mineral/milk/cheese/yoghurt. **6 marks**
6. Cartilage/upwards/downwards/around/ossification. **5 marks**
7. Epiphysis/shaft/periosteum. **3 marks**

Total 28 marks

Bones (page 59)
1. Scapula/flat/protection. **3 marks**
2. Clavicle. **1 mark**
3. Long bones/humerus/ulna/ radius. **4 marks**
4. Metacarpal/phalanges/carpal. **3 marks**
5. Femur/tibia/fibula/patella. **4 marks**
6. Heart/lungs. **1 mark**
7. Irregular/spinal cord/cervical/thoracic/five/lumbar/sacrum/coccyx/pelvis. **9 marks**

Total 25 marks

Joints (page 63)
1. Two or more. **1 mark**
2. Hyaline cartilage/elastic/protects/rubbing/joint capsule/synovial membrane/synovial fluid/lubricates. **8 marks**
3. Ball and socket/rotation/extension/flexion. **4 marks**
4. Hinge/flexion/extension/planta/dorsi. **5 marks**
5. Rotates/flex/adduction/flexion/extension/atlas/axis. **7 marks**

Total 25 marks

Muscles (page 69)
1.

Type of muscle	voluntary	involuntary	cardiac	
Example	biceps	gut	heart	
Type of muscle fibre	cylindrical	spindle-shaped	interlaced	**10 marks**

2. Fast twitch/slow twitch. **2 marks**
3. Ends/friction. **2 marks**
4. Tendon/origin/insertion. **3 marks**
5. The muscle cells do not all rest at the same time; even when we are asleep some are ready for action. **1 mark**
6. Trapezius – triangle shape below the neck on the back.
Latissimus dorsi – across the back below the trapezius.
Pectoralis major – front of the chest across the breast bone. **3 marks**
7. Location – stomach. Exercise – sit-ups. **2 marks**
8. Muscles working in pairs. One relaxes when the other contracts. **1 mark**
9. Basketball jump shot: arm bends to prepare and straightens to shoot.
Biceps bends the arm; triceps straightens the arm.
Football kicking the ball: the hamstring causes the knee to bend to prepare to kick the ball; the quadricep straightens the knee to cause the kicking action. **6 marks**

Total 30 marks

Flexibility, risk assessment and posture (page 77)

1. Range/movement.   **2 marks**
2. Teresa, Derek, Albert (3 marks). Teresa is female; she and Derek are younger than Albert (2 marks).   **5 marks**
3. To prevent injury.   **1 mark**
4. Cricket. Voluntary = pads, gloves, box. Compulsory = helmet.   **3 marks**
5. Any three similar answers to the example.   **3 marks**
6. Single sex = rugby.
   Mixed = badminton doubles.
   Open competition = table tennis.   **3 marks**
7. A sign is what you can see, feel, hear or smell.
   A symptom is what the casualty can feel and tells you.   **2 marks**
8. Break/dislocation.   **2 marks**
9. Break.   **1 mark**
       Total 22 marks

Flexibility, risk assessment and posture (page 78)

1. Inside the elbow.   **1 mark**
2. Pain, swelling.   **2 marks**
3. Open.   **1 mark**
4. Dislocation.   **1 mark**
5. Special gloves.   **1 mark**
6. Hypothermia.   **1 mark**
7. Shivering/skin cold and pale.   **2 marks**
8. Take on plenty of fluid.   **1 mark**
9. Tiredness/nausea/dizziness (any two).   **2 marks**
10. Loss of consciousness is a result of some interference with the function of the brain.   **1 mark**
11. Danger/response/airway/breathing/circulation.   **5 marks**
12. Unconsciousness/cold/high pulse rate (any two).   **2 marks**
13. Overweight/lacks strength/low back pain.   **3 marks**
14. Being able to elegantly maintain the relative position of the body parts.   **1 mark**
15. Yoga.   **1 mark**
       Total 25 marks

Motor skills and drugs in sport (page 84)

1. Check answers against motor skill definitions on pages 79-80.   **12 marks**
2. Check answers against motor skill definitions on pages 79-80.   **2 marks**
3. Expected and welcome physical and/or psychological effects.   **1 mark**
4. Cancer.   **1 mark**
5. Damages the heart, damages the ability of the blood to carry oxygen, damages the blood vessels, increases blood pressure (any three).   **3 marks**
6. Damages the alveoli in the lungs.   **1 mark**
7. C Cirrhosis   **1 mark**
8. To win, to compete at the highest level, to make a lot of money, to be famous (any one).   **1 mark**
9. Prohibited substances/prohibited methods.   **2 marks**
10. To win, to compete at the highest level, to make a lot of money, to be famous (any one).   **1 mark**
11. Insomnia, irregular heartbeat, increased heart rate, high blood pressure (any one).   **1 mark**
12. Narcotic.   **1 mark**
13. Anabolic steroid.   **1 mark**
14. Human growth hormone.   **1 mark**
15. International Olympic Committee.   **1 mark**
       Total 30 marks